JAMES MARTIN

more
HOME
COMFORTS

100 new recipes from the tv series

PHOTOGRAPHY BY PETER CASSIDY

quadrille

Fudge:
In lasting memory of my best mate,
rest in peace fella, I will miss you.

Publishing director: Sarah Lavelle
Creative director: Helen Lewis
Art direction and design: Gabriella Le Grazie
Photographer: Peter Cassidy
Project editor: Laura Herring
Food stylists: Janet Brinkworth, David Birt, Chris Start…
    and James Martin
Props stylist: Rebecca Newport
Home economist: Janet Brinkworth
Production controller: Tom Moore
Production director: Vincent Smith

First published in 2016 by
Quadrille Publishing Limited
www.quadrille.co.uk

Quadrille is an imprint of Hardie Grant
www.hardiegrant.com.au

Text © James Martin 2016
Photography © Peter Cassidy 2016
Design and layout © Quadrille Publishing Limited 2016

The rights of the author have been asserted.

Cataloguing in Publication Data: a catalogue record for
this book is available from the British Library.

978 1 84949 791 6
Printed in China

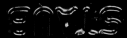

Contents

Introduction

When this, the second *Home Comforts* book, hits the shelves I will be able to say I've been working in the business for more than 20 years. As a young kid I never thought I would be doing this for a living, so I want to take this chance to say a huge thank you for all your support and for making my dream come true.

Food is such a massive subject that in some ways I really feel I haven't even scratched the surface yet, but over the years I've been lucky enough to have worked with some amazing people and in some of the best kitchens around, so I've packed this book full of the hints, tips and shortcuts I've learnt along the way. Food should be enjoyed in the eating and the cooking – let's face it, none of us wants to spend hours behind the stove sweating to make lunch and supper – it's all about making life easier. From great simple starters to main courses that will impress at the dinner table to desserts I can't resist, this book is full of all the foods I really love to cook at home. It's food that is accessible to all.

The art of making great food was taught to me at a young age as I watched my mum cooking great food that we produced on the farm. Good ingredients are still really important to me – I have used some great British suppliers in these recipes, and my vegetable garden has got a lot of use, too.

It was such a pleasure working with amazingly talented chefs on the TV series, like Pierre Koffmann, Mary Berry and Michael Caines. They all helped at the stove, making fantastic, simple food that you can enjoy at home. I loved working with them; there is nothing better than sharing time with friends and family – that's the real essence of home comforts.

So as I turn off the stove at home as we finish this second book, I hope you enjoy it as much as the first. It's got everything in it I love: great ingredients, fab food and great stories. And, of course, my two dogs, Ralph and Fudge, who also enjoyed the process, proving that home comforts should be for everybody.

Enjoy!

Instant Comforts

Beetroot salad with buffalo curd cheese

I grow my own beetroots in the garden and think they pair really well with the curd cheese in this recipe. Buffalo milk is so rich and creamy, which means you get loads of curd, and it has an amazing flavour too. Give this salad a go, it's so easy to make and looks great.

Serves 4

5 raw beetroots, tops on
2 litres buffalo milk
50ml lemon juice
90ml extra virgin olive oil
½ baguette, cut into small chunks
2 sprigs of rosemary, leaves picked
2 sprigs of thyme, leaves picked
2 tablespoons sherry vinegar
1 teaspoon cumin seeds
1 tablespoon tarragon leaves
1 tablespoon oregano leaves, plus extra to garnish
1 tablespoon marjoram leaves
1 tablespoon chopped flat-leaf parsley leaves
sea salt and freshly ground black pepper
4 sprigs of edible flowers (optional)
4 sprigs of dill

Cut the leaves from the tops of the beetroots and set aside. Place the beetroots in a saucepan half filled with water, bring to the boil, and simmer for 30–45 minutes until tender when pierced with a knife. Set aside to cool.

Place the buffalo milk in a saucepan and bring to the boil, without stirring. When it is just about to boil, whisk in the lemon juice – you will immediately see a reaction as the milk solidifies and separates into curds and whey. Carefully pour it through a sieve set over a bowl and allow to drain for 5 minutes. The longer you leave it to drain, the more solid a cheese you will get.

Heat a frying pan until hot, then add 50ml of the olive oil and the bread. Add the rosemary and thyme, and fry until golden brown and just crispy. Tip straight into a bowl, along with the oil from the pan and the sherry vinegar.

Add 2 tablespoons of the oil to the pan, then add the cumin seeds and beetroot tops, and cook until just wilted. Add to the croutons.

Peel the beetroot and cut into chunks, then add to the bowl along with the tarragon, oregano, marjoram and parsley, and mix well. Season with salt and pepper, then spoon onto serving plates.

Top with spoonfuls of the curd, a drizzle of olive oil, and the sprigs of oregano, edible flowers, if using, and dill.

Hazelnut and Parmesan-crusted chicken

The key to this dish is to cook the chicken in plenty of butter. It will colour the meat while keeping it moist. Using just oil can cause it to burn before it's cooked through. You can use almonds as well as, or instead of, the hazelnuts if you wish.

Serves 4

4 boneless skinless chicken breasts
40g hazelnuts
25g Parmesan cheese, freshly grated
2 lemons, zested, then cut in half
2 sprigs of thyme, leaves picked
40g panko breadcrumbs
75g plain flour
sea salt and freshly ground black pepper
2 eggs, beaten
250g unsalted butter
2 heads of little gem lettuce, leaves
   separated

Put the chicken between two pieces of greaseproof paper and bat out with a rolling pin to about 1cm thick.

Place the hazelnuts, Parmesan, lemon zest and thyme in a food processor, and blitz to fine crumbs. Add the breadcrumbs and pulse quickly to just break them up, then tip out onto a plate.

Season the flour with salt and pepper, then dust the chicken with the flour. Dip into the beaten egg, then into the hazelnut breadcrumbs, making sure to coat each side of the chicken thoroughly.

Heat the butter in a large frying pan, then add the chicken breasts and fry until golden – about 5 minutes on each side – basting with the butter as you go. Drain on some kitchen paper, then finish with a little more Parmesan.

Lay the chicken on serving plates, drizzle over all the remaining butter in the frying pan and finish with a squeeze of lemon juice. Pile the lettuce leaves alongside, with a wedge of lemon.

Keralan prawns

Serves 4

2 tablespoons vegetable oil
1 teaspoon black onion seeds
10 curry leaves
2 teaspoons ground cumin
½ teaspoon ground turmeric
½ teaspoon fenugreek seeds
1 onion, finely chopped
2 garlic cloves, finely chopped
2 green chillies, finely chopped
2 teaspoon finely chopped ginger
1 tablespoon tamarind paste
160ml coconut cream
150ml chicken or vegetable stock
400g raw tiger prawns, peeled and deveined
sea salt and freshly ground black pepper

To serve

4 naan, roti or paratha breads
1 lime, juiced
2 tablespoons roughly chopped coriander leaves

Preheat the oven to 200°C/400°F/gas mark 6.

Heat a large wok until just smoking. Add the vegetable oil, black onion seeds and curry leaves, and stir-fry until the seeds pop. Add the spices and fry for 1 minute, then add the onion, garlic, chillies and ginger, and fry over a medium heat for 10 minutes, until softened.

Add the tamarind, coconut cream and stock, and bring to the boil, then turn the heat down and simmer for another 10 minutes, until the onion is soft.

Toss in the prawns, coating them in the sauce, and cook for 3–4 minutes, until they have cooked through and changed colour.

While the prawns are cooking, place the breads in the oven to warm through.

Add the lime juice and coriander to the prawns, then taste and season with salt and pepper, if necessary. Cook for 1 minute, then serve on top of the warmed bread.

Chicken and Serrano ham croquetas with Padrón peppers

When I do get away, which to be fair isn't very often, one of the places I head to is Spain. I love their attitude towards food. Sure, the Italians are good, but they do like to shout about it, whereas I feel the Spanish just let the ingredients do the talking. One trip to the famous market of La Boqueria in Barcelona is proof of that. It's the best market I've been to, and in it are the best tapas bars. This dish comes from there.

Serves 4

75g unsalted butter
150g plain flour
450ml milk
sea salt and freshly ground black pepper
75g jamón Serrano, roughly chopped
75g cooked chicken, chopped
1 small bunch of parsley, leaves picked and roughly chopped
25g flaked toasted almonds
2 eggs, beaten
75g fresh breadcrumbs
vegetable oil, for deep-frying
4 tablespoons olive oil
200g Padrón peppers
½ teaspoon sea salt

Melt the butter in a large saucepan, then whisk in 75g of the flour and cook for 30 seconds. Whisk in the milk slowly until you have a very thick sauce – almost the consistency of mashed potato. Season with salt and pepper.

Tip into a bowl and stir in the jamón Serrano, chicken and parsley. Season with salt and pepper, then stir in the flaked almonds. Place in the fridge to chill for 10 minutes until just firm.

Wet your hands, then take spoonfuls of the mixture and roll them into balls.

Place the remaining 75g of flour, the eggs and breadcrumbs in separate bowls, and season with salt and pepper. Roll the balls first in the flour, then in the eggs, then in the breadcrumbs, then place on a work surface and roll gently into cylinder shapes. Set aside while you heat the oil and fry the peppers.

Heat a deep-fat fryer to 170°C/340°F, or heat the oil for deep-frying in a deep heavy-based frying pan until a breadcrumb sizzles and turns brown when dropped into it. (CAUTION: hot oil can be dangerous. Do not leave unattended.)

While the oil is heating up, heat a frying pan until hot, then add the olive oil, Padrón peppers and half the salt, and fry for 2–3 minutes, until just golden and softened. Tip into a serving bowl and sprinkle with the last of the salt.

Deep-fry the croquetas in batches for 3–4 minutes, until golden-brown and hot through. Remove and drain on kitchen paper.

Serve the croquetas with the Padrón peppers.

Hot paper bag pastrami, fontina and pickled cucumber sarnie with parsnip and carrot crisps

The team thought I was going mad when I made this. I wanted an old army ammo tin to cook it in, but the producers of the show would only let me go so far. Pastrami is an amazing thing to see being made – the meat is coated in a rub to cure it, then smoked, then steamed to produce that fantastic flavour.

Serves 4

150ml rice wine or cider vinegar

50g caster sugar

2 teaspoons sea salt

1 teaspoon yellow mustard seeds

1 cucumber, thinly sliced

1 small bunch of dill, roughly chopped

12 slices wheat 'n' rye sourdough bread

40g softened unsalted butter

1 tablespoon Dijon mustard

300g thinly sliced pastrami

400g sliced fontina cheese

vegetable oil, for deep-frying

3 parsnips, peeled into ribbons

3 carrots, peeled into ribbons

sea salt and freshly ground black pepper

Preheat the oven to 200°C/400°F/gas mark 6.

Put the rice wine vinegar, sugar, salt and mustard seeds into a saucepan, and heat until simmering and the sugar has dissolved. Put the cucumber into a bowl and pour the hot vinegar mixture over the top, add the dill, then stir well and set aside to infuse.

Meanwhile, toast all the sourdough bread and spread with butter. Lay four slices on a board, butter-side up, and spread with a little mustard. Top with half the pastrami, then half the cheese and a layer of pickled cucumber. Place a second piece of bread on top of each sandwich, spread with mustard, and repeat the layers of pastrami, cheese and pickled cucumber. Top with the last piece of bread so you have four three-storey sandwiches.

Take four large sheets of baking parchment and wrap each sandwich individually in the parchment, then secure with string. Place the parcels on a baking sheet in the oven and bake for 10 minutes, until hot through.

Heat a deep-fat fryer to 160°C/320°F, or heat the oil for deep-frying in a deep heavy-based frying pan until a breadcrumb sizzles and turns brown when dropped into it. (CAUTION: hot oil can be dangerous. Do not leave unattended.)

Carefully lower the parsnip and carrot peelings into the oil in batches, and fry for 4–5 minutes, until crispy but not browned – you want to dry the peelings out, without letting them get burnt. Drain on kitchen paper and toss with salt.

Serve the hot sandwiches with a pile of parsnip and carrot crisps.

Pea soup with Parmesan

So simple! Using peas from the freezer, this soup can be made in minutes. It's fresh and full of colour. A few pieces of soft cheese – like ricotta or feta – are also good scattered on top.

Serves 4

25g unsaltd butter

2 banana shallots, finely chopped

400g frozen peas

350ml chicken or vegetable stock

150ml double cream

3 heaped tablespoons freshly grated
 Parmesan cheese

sea salt and freshly ground black pepper

Heat a sauté pan until hot, then add the butter and shallots, and sweat for 2–3 minutes, until the shallots have just softened.

Add the peas and stock, and bring to the boil, then reduce the heat and simmer for 2–3 minutes, until the peas are just hot through. Add the cream and Parmesan, and bring to a simmer.

Remove from the heat, carefully pour into a blender and blitz to a smooth purée. Return the soup to the saucepan and season with a touch of salt and plenty of pepper.

Pork tenderloin with prunes and Armagnac

This is one of those dishes that I used to cook a lot when I was younger. It's only now that I realise just how good it was and still is! It's so quick to make – and it tasted even better made with the prunes I had hiding in the back of the cupboard, soaked in some Armagnac.

Serves 4

1kg floury potatoes, peeled and cut into chunks
200g unsalted butter
325ml double cream
sea salt and freshly ground black pepper
1 pork tenderloin fillet, cut into 12 thick slices
1 shallot, finely chopped
75ml Armagnac
150ml chicken stock
16 stoned prunes

Place the potatoes in a pan of cold, salted water and bring to the boil, then reduce the heat and simmer for 12–15 minutes, or until tender. Drain the potatoes in a colander and return to the pan, then place over a low heat for a couple of minutes to dry them slightly.

Tip the potatoes back into the colander and then pass them through a ricer. Add 150g of the butter and 150ml of the cream, and beat to form a very smooth mash, then season to taste with salt and pepper. Set aside to keep warm.

Place the pieces of pork fillet on a clingfilm-lined board, cover with more clingfilm and bash until 1cm thick. Discard the clingfilm and season with salt and pepper.

Heat a frying pan until hot, then add a knob of the butter and the pork slices and fry on each side for 1–2 minutes until golden and only just cooked through. Remove and place on a plate.

Add the rest of the butter and sweat the shallot for 1 minute, then add the Armagnac and flambé.

Add the stock and the rest of the cream, and bring to a simmer, then add the prunes and return the pork and any juices to the pan. Cook for another 2 minutes, until the pork is cooked through.

Spoon the sauce over the pork fillet and serve the mash alongside.

Tomato tarts with blowtorched salad

Simple flavours are always the best, and fresh tomatoes from the greenhouse are the epitome of this. Warming them gently with a blowtorch is a great way to serve them in a salad, just with a simple dressing. The great thing about these tomato tarts is that you can freeze them, wrapped in greaseproof paper, and cook them straight from frozen.

Serves 4

For the tarts

500g all-butter puff pastry
1 egg yolk, beaten
200g Gruyère cheese, grated
400g mixed heritage tomatoes, thickly sliced
sea salt and freshly ground black pepper
4 sprigs of thyme, leaves picked
1 tablespoon rapeseed oil

For the salad

300g mixed heritage tomatoes
1 red onion, thickly sliced
2 heads of romaine lettuce, cut into thick slices
4 tablespoons vegetable oil
1 tablespoon white wine vinegar
1 tablespoon Dijon mustard
1 egg yolk

Preheat the oven to 220°C/425°F/gas mark 7.

Roll the pastry into a large square, about 3mm thick, then cut out four 17.5cm circles and place on a baking tray. Mark a border with a knife about a little finger's width in from the edge, then brush with the beaten egg yolk.

Pile the grated cheese in the centre of each disc, leaving the border free of cheese. Lay the tomatoes in a circle on top of the cheese. Season the tarts with salt and pepper, then scatter the thyme leaves over the top, drizzle with rapeseed oil and bake for 15 minutes, until golden brown and cooked through.

Meanwhile, make the salad. Place the tomatoes, red onion and lettuce in a roasting tray and drizzle over a little of the vegetable oil. Toss to combine, then char with a blowtorch or under a hot grill until caramelised – about 4–5 minutes.

Put the vinegar, mustard, egg yolk and the rest of the vegetable oil into a jam jar with a lid and shake well until emulsified. Season with salt and pepper. Drizzle just enough of the dressing over the salad to coat.

Pile the salad into a bowl and serve alongside the tarts. The remaining dressing will keep in the sealed jar in the fridge for up to one week.

Roasted sardines and mackerel with radishes

I love my wood-fired oven, but this also can be done on a tray in a barbecue with a lid. The idea is to get it really hot and to get a nice smoky taste going on in the fish.

6 ripe tomatoes, cut into chunks

4 sprigs of thyme, leaves picked

3 garlic cloves, crushed

1 baguette, torn into pieces

125ml extra virgin olive oil

sea salt and freshly ground black pepper

8 sardines, gutted and cleaned

4 mackerel, gutted and cleaned, cut into large chunks

2 bunches of radishes, trimmed

1 teaspoon cumin seeds

2 tablespoons clear honey

1 small bunch of basil, leaves picked

Preheat the oven to 200°C/400°F/gas mark 6.

Place the tomatoes, thyme, garlic and baguette pieces in a roasting tray and drizzle with 75ml of the oil. Season with salt and pepper, then roast until the bread is charred around the edges.

Meanwhile, place the sardines stomach-down on a board and press gently down the length of the fish. Flip over and cut through the backbone at the tail and head, then, using your fingers, peel the bones out, leaving the fish boneless.

Remove the tomatoes from the oven, then turn the heat up as high as it will go and lightly oil a baking tray. Lay the mackerel, sardines and radishes on the tray, scatter the cumin seeds over, then drizzle the honey and 2 tablespoons of the olive oil over the top. Roast for 5–10 minutes, until the fish is cooked through.

Tear the basil and scatter over the roasted tomatoes and bread. Crush the tomatoes lightly.

Pile the roasted tomatoes and bread onto serving plates and top with the fish and radishes. Drizzle over the last of the olive oil.

Salmon and sorrel with vermouth

This classic combination is one that I first did in France as a young apprentice chef. The flavour of sorrel is amazing – slightly bitter but fresh and lemony. This dish is all about the sorrel – overcook it and it can become a little too bitter. It's easy to grow, and you can find it in most garden centres in the herb section. It's great raw, just ripped or chopped into salads.

Serves 2

40g unsalted butter, for greasing
sea salt and freshly ground black pepper
200g salmon fillet, cut into 8 thin slices
1 shallot, finely sliced
75ml vermouth
75ml white wine
150ml double cream
75g sorrel leaves, deveined and very finely sliced
1 bag of salad leaves
50ml house dressing (see below)

For the house dressing

1 egg yolk
1 teaspoon English mustard
2 teaspoons clear honey
2 tablespoons cider vinegar
150ml vegetable oil
1 banana shallot, finely chopped
1 garlic clove, finely chopped
1 tablespoon finely chopped flat-leaf parsley leaves
1 tablespoon finely chopped mint leaves
1 tablespoon finely chopped basil leaves
1 tablespoon finely chopped thyme leaves
salt and freshly ground black pepper

To make the house dressing, place the egg yolk in a bowl with the mustard and honey. Add the cider vinegar and whisk, then gradually add the vegetable oil, whisking all the time until thick and creamy. Add the shallot, garlic, parsley, mint, basil and thyme, and whisk once more, then season with salt and pepper, and set aside.

Preheat the grill to high. Butter an oven tray all over the base, then season with salt and pepper. Lay the salmon slices on the tray in two batches of four overlapping slices, then set aside.

Heat a frying pan until hot. Add the shallot, vermouth and white wine, and cook for about 5 minutes, until reduced by half. Add the double cream and cook the sauce for 2–3 minutes until reduced and thickened.

Meanwhile, put the salmon under the grill for 3 minutes until just cooked through.

Season the sauce to taste with salt and pepper, then remove from the heat and stir in the sorrel. Spoon onto a serving plate and carefully lay the salmon slices on top.

Toss the salad leaves with some of the dressing and serve alongside. The rest of the dressing will keep in a jar in the fridge for a few days.

Lemon chicken, black bean squid and stir-fried rice

These are my favourites among the dishes that I order from my local Chinese restaurant. They make them properly, without MSG or any other unnecessary stuff, just simple clean flavours – that's the essence of Chinese cooking for me.

Place the chicken in a bowl, then mix the soy sauce, honey and cornflour together in a separate bowl and pour over the chicken. Toss to coat, then set aside while you prepare all the vegetables and herbs. Mix the lemon zest, juice and chicken stock together.

Mix the squid, sesame oil, soy sauce and mirin together in a bowl and set aside for 5 minutes.

To cook the lemon chicken, heat a wok or frying pan until hot and add the groundnut oil. Add the sherry to the chicken and stir through, then put into the hot wok and stir-fry for 2 minutes, until just sealed. Add the chilli, garlic and ginger, and the lemon and chicken stock, and bring to the boil, stirring well. Reduce the heat to a simmer and cook for 4–5 minutes, until the chicken is cooked through and the sauce has thickened. Remove from the wok and transfer to a bowl. Cover with clingfilm, and keep warm.

To make the stir-fried rice, clean the wok or frying pan and reheat until hot. Add the groundnut oil and when it's shimmering, add the rice and stir-fry for 1 minute before adding the spring onions, coriander, soy sauce and sesame oil. Stir-fry for 2–3 minutes until piping hot right through, then tip into a serving bowl, cover with clingfilm, and keep warm.

To cook the black bean squid, clean the wok or frying pan again, then reheat until hot. Add the groundnut oil, and when it's shimmering add the ginger, garlic and chillies and stir-fry for 2 minutes, until just softened. Add the marinated squid and the black beans and stir-fry for 2–3 minutes over a high heat. Add the chicken stock, sherry, spring onions and coriander, stir well, then simmer for another couple of minutes until the squid is cooked through.

Add the spring onions to the chicken, and serve with the black bean squid and stir-fried rice.

Serves 4

For the chicken

400g boneless skinless chicken breast, cut into strips

2 tablespoons light soy sauce

1 tablespoon clear honey

2 tablespoon cornflour

2 lemons, zested and juiced

75ml chicken stock

1 teaspoon groundnut oil

1 tablespoon dry sherry

1 red chilli, finely chopped

3 garlic cloves, finely sliced

2cm piece of ginger, peeled and finely grated

3 spring onions, finely sliced

For the squid

300g squid, cleaned and cut into strips

1 teaspoon sesame oil

1 tablespoon soy sauce

1 tablespoon mirin

2 tablespoons groundnut oil

3cm piece of ginger, peeled and finely chopped

2 garlic cloves, finely chopped

2 red chillies, finely chopped

40g black beans, rinsed, drained and roughly chopped

50–75ml chicken stock

2 tablespoons dry sherry or Shaoxing rice wine

3 spring onions, finely sliced

2–3 tablespoons roughly chopped coriander

For the stir-fried rice

1 tablespoon groundnut oil

300g cooked and cooled basmati rice

2 spring onions, sliced

2 tablespoons coriander leaves, roughly chopped

2 tablespoons soy sauce

1 teaspoon sesame oil

Pan-fried black pudding with scallops and ginger purée

As there are so few ingredients here, you need to make sure you get really good-quality black pudding and scallops. Be careful with the ginger purée, as it can pack a pretty hot and spicy punch!

Serves 4

200g ginger, peeled and thinly sliced
4 curry leaves
75g palm sugar
50g tamarind paste
a pinch of sea salt
25g caster sugar
1 apple, cut into 12 thin slices
10g unsalted butter
8 thin slices of pancetta
8 x 1cm thick slices of black pudding
4 large scallops, with roe
1 teaspoon olive oil
½ lemon, juiced
4 teaspoons extra virgin olive oil

Put 500ml of water into a sauté pan and set on the heat. Add the ginger, curry leaves, palm sugar, tamarind and salt, and bring to the boil, then simmer for 10 minutes. Cool slightly, then place in a blender and blitz to a fine purée.

Put the caster sugar into a frying pan and heat until just golden, then add the apple slices and cook in the caramel for a few seconds before adding the butter. Add a splash of water and swirl around so that the apple is coated with a light caramel.

Heat a non-stick frying pan until very hot, then add the pancetta and cook on both sides until crispy. Remove from the pan and set aside, then add the black pudding to the pan. Fry on each side for 30 seconds only, until just crispy but still soft on the inside. Remove and set aside.

Drizzle the scallops with the olive oil and sear for 1½ minutes on each side until golden and just cooked. Squeeze the lemon juice over the top and remove from the pan.

Cut the scallops in half widthways. Place a piece of caramelised apple in the centre of each plate. Top with a small spoonful of ginger purée, then a piece of black pudding, then half a scallop, and repeat with another piece of apple, the purée, black pudding, scallop and apple, finishing with a final spoonful of the purée.

Finally, add a couple of pieces of crispy pancetta and drizzle with the extra virgin olive oil.

Côte de boeuf with béarnaise sauce

A dish for a legend. When Sir Stirling Moss wanted to learn how to make béarnaise sauce, who was I to say otherwise? And with a côte de boeuf – which is one of the best cuts of meat out there – it creates the best-tasting plate of food there is. Purists will say that the shallots should be strained out, but I like to keep them in. While working for some of the greatest chefs in the world, I saw that they kept the shallots in, and I agree.

Serves 4

1.8kg côte de boeuf

4 large chipping potatoes, peeled and cut into 1cm thick batons

vegetable oil or dripping, for deep-frying

300g unsalted butter

1 small banana shallot, finely chopped

½ teaspoon white peppercorns

3 tablespoons tarragon vinegar

2 egg yolks

1 small bunch of tarragon, leaves picked and finely chopped

sea salt and freshly ground black pepper

1 bunch of watercress, picked

Preheat the oven to 180°C/350°F/gas mark 4. Place the beef on an oven tray and roast for 30–40 minutes until cooked to your liking.

While the beef is cooking, prepare the chips. Heat a deep-fat fryer to 140°C/285°F, or heat the oil for deep-frying in a deep heavy-based frying pan until a breadcrumb sizzles and turns just a very pale gold when dropped into it. (CAUTION: hot oil can be dangerous. Do not leave unattended.) Carefully place the chips in the oil in batches and fry for 4–5 minutes until pale but tender. Remove and drain on kitchen paper. When the beef is nearly ready, turn the oil up to 190°C/375°F.

Remove the beef from the oven and let it rest for 5–10 minutes.

Heat a large frying pan until hot and add 50g of the butter. When it's foaming, add the beef and sear on each side for 1 minute until browned, spooning the butter over the top. Remove from the pan and let it rest on a plate while you make the béarnaise.

Place the rest of the butter in a pan and heat until melted, then skim off any foam. Place the shallot, peppercorns and vinegar in a small saucepan and bring to the boil. Simmer over a low heat for a few minutes until the liquid has evaporated and there is only 1 tablespoon left.

Put the egg yolks into a bowl and whisk together. Whisk in the melted butter, a little at a time initially, then in a thin constant stream, whisking all the time – you want the mixture to emulsify and thicken slightly. Don't add the solids at the bottom of the melted butter – discard them. When all the butter has been added, spoon in the shallot and any liquid, add the chopped tarragon, and season to taste with salt and pepper.

When ready to serve, return the chips to the hot oil and cook for 3–4 minutes until golden and crispy. Drain on kitchen paper, sprinkle with salt and serve immediately.

Carve the beef and lay the slices on a plate. Pile the chips alongside, and finish with a dollop of béarnaise and the watercress.

Veal escalopes with salsa verde

When everyone gets bored with sausages and burgers, try this and you might never go back. Veal is the perfect meat for the barbecue. It can be cooked just like steak, but the key to cooking this particular cut of meat well is not to overcook it, as it's very lean and can easily dry out.

Serves 6–8

5 lemons
1 small bunch of mint
1 small bunch of flat-leaf parsley
½ small bunch of dill
½ small bunch of chervil
1 small bunch of tarragon
1 bulb of garlic, cut in half, plus 2 garlic cloves
250ml extra virgin olive oil
1kg veal cushion, cut into 2cm thick slices
1 shallot, finely chopped
2 sprigs of basil
3 anchovies, finely chopped
1 tablespoon Dijon mustard
1 tablespoon capers, drained
sea salt and freshly ground black pepper
300g spinach leaves

Heat a barbecue until the coals are glowing, or heat a griddle pan until very hot.

Zest 2 of the lemons into a large bowl and squeeze in the juice. Add a few sprigs of mint, parsley, dill, chervil and tarragon, and the halved garlic bulb. Add 150ml of the extra virgin olive oil, mix to combine and set aside.

Place a long sheet of clingfilm on a board, then lay all the slices of veal on it and cover with a second sheet of clingfilm. Bash with a rolling pin until about 1cm thick, then place the pieces of veal in the herby oil. Toss to coat, then set aside while you make the salsa verde.

Chop the shallot, garlic cloves and the remaining herbs, including the basil, together finely on a board. Add the zest of 2 more lemons, then chop again. Add the anchovies and chop all together, then finally add the Dijon mustard and capers, and chop until you have a fine mixture. Season with salt and pepper, then make a hollow in the centre.

Lift the veal out of the marinade and onto the barbecue or griddle and cook for 2–3 minutes, then turn over and cook for another 2 minutes. Remove and put straight onto a serving platter.

While the veal cooks, heat a sauté pan until hot. Add 50ml of the extra virgin olive oil and the spinach leaves, and sauté until just wilted, then spoon over the veal.

Pour the last of the extra virgin olive oil into the centre of the herb pile and mix together until it forms a thick paste. Spoon over the top of the veal and spinach, and serve with the last lemon, cut into wedges.

Salmon and charred sweetcorn salsa

It's taken ten years to master the art of growing sweetcorn in my garden, and all we really did was move the plants round from year to year to see where it grew best. We now have the perfect site. The problem now is that the dog has got a taste for it too, so he's forever pulling the plants up.

Serves 4

4 whole corn on the cob, outer husks removed

6 spring onions, trimmed

2 red chillies

3 limes, cut in half

2 tablespoons roughly chopped coriander, stems and leaves

5 tablespoons extra virgin olive oil

sea salt and freshly ground black pepper

4 x 100g salmon fillets, boneless and skinless

Put the corn on the cob into a large pan of water, set over a high heat and bring to the boil, then turn the heat down and simmer for 15 minutes until tender.

Meanwhile, heat a griddle pan until hot. Add the spring onions and chillies, and char on each side for a couple of minutes, until just blackened. Remove and roughly chop.

Add the limes to the griddle pan, cut-side down, and char for 1 minute until just blackened. Remove and set aside.

When the corn is tender, drain and set on the griddle pan to char – keep an eye on it as you don't want one side very black! Turn every couple of minutes so that it is evenly charred. Remove from the griddle, then cut 2 cobs in half and set aside.

Remove the kernels from the other 2 cobs and place in a food processor along with the chopped spring onions, chillies and coriander. Squeeze in the juice from 1 lime and add 2 tablespoons of the olive oil, then pulse until everything is roughly chopped. Season to taste with salt and pepper.

Rub each side of the salmon fillets with a little of the olive oil, then place on the griddle pan and char on each side for 1 minute until just cooked through.

Place on plates with a spoonful of the salsa, half a charred corn on the cob and a piece of lime. Finish with the last of the olive oil, drizzled over.

Parma ham and goat's cheese en croute with chilli apple chutney

The simplest ingredients often taste the best, and this is a great example of that. I'm not much of a fan of goat's cheese but I do like the milder types that aren't chalky. If you're not sure, give it a try!

Serves 2

For the goat's cheese en croute

2 tablespoons unsalted butter
100g baby spinach leaves
grated nutmeg
sea salt and freshly ground black pepper
4 slices of Parma ham
200g unrinded soft goat's cheese, cut into 4 discs
325g puff pastry, rolled out to 3mm thick
1 egg, beaten
green salad, to serve

For the chutney

100g dark muscovado sugar
1 shallot, finely chopped
2cm piece of ginger, peeled and finely chopped
1 teaspoon mixed spice
½ teaspoon dried chilli flakes
2 apples, grated
150g sultanas
150ml white wine vinegar

Preheat the oven to 200°C/400°F/gas mark 6.

Heat a frying pan until hot, then add the butter and spinach, and cook until just wilted. Season with nutmeg, salt and pepper, then tip out onto a paper-lined plate and leave to cool.

Wrap the Parma ham around the cheese to cover it on all sides.

Divide the pastry into eight equal rectangles and place the spinach on top of four of them. Place the cheese on top and season well. Brush the edge of the pastry with the some of the egg and top with the remaining pieces of pastry. Press down lightly around the edges, then crimp the edges. Brush with the remaining eggwash and place on a baking tray. Bake for 20 minutes until cooked through and golden brown.

To make the chutney, heat a saucepan until medium hot, then add the sugar and cook until just melted, stirring occasionally. Add all the remaining ingredients and cook for 15–20 minutes until the apples are tender and the chutney has thickened slightly.

Remove from the heat and cool slightly, then serve with the goat's cheese en croute and a green salad.

Singapore chilli crab with egg noodles

The aptly named Crab Under the Bridge, in Singapore, is where I tried this for the first time, and I loved it as much then as I do now. It's not food for a fancy dinner party – it's food for getting messy, and you need a bib and tea towels as you pick the meat from the shells. The keys to it are the spices and the stickiness, and to spend as much time eating the crab as you do licking your fingers.

Serves 2–3

2 tablespoons vegetable oil

10cm piece of ginger, peeled and finely chopped

3 garlic cloves, chopped

3 red bird's-eye chillies, finely chopped

4 spring onions, roughly chopped, tops and bottoms kept separate

225ml tomato ketchup

125ml sweet chilli sauce

125ml hoisin sauce

1½ tablespoons fish sauce

3 tablespoons soy sauce

2 tablespoons caster sugar

200g fine egg noodles

1kg whole crab

2 tablespoons roughly chopped mint leaves

2 tablespoons roughly chopped coriander leaves

Heat a wok until hot, then add the vegetable oil, ginger, garlic and chillies, and stir-fry for 2 minutes. Add the chopped tops of the spring onions and stir-fry for another minute. Add the tomato, sweet chilli, hoisin, fish and soy sauces and the sugar, then bring to the boil. Reduce the heat to a simmer and cook for 5 minutes. Transfer three ladlefuls of the sauce to a bowl and set aside.

Meanwhile, cook the noodles according to the packet instructions and drain in a sieve.

Chop the crab into large pieces. Remove and discard the dead men's fingers, then crack the claws lightly. Add the crab to the wok of simmering sauce and toss to coat thoroughly, then simmer for 5 minutes. Transfer to a serving bowl, cover with clingfilm and keep warm.

Clean the wok or frying pan and return to the heat. Add the reserved three ladlefuls of sauce, and when it's simmering, add the cooked drained noodles, three-quarters of the remaining chopped spring onions, the mint and coriander, and toss to combine and heat through.

Serve the crab in a large bowl, garnished with the rest of the spring onions and with the noodles in a separate bowl.

Chicken curry with basmati rice

This is better than any takeaway, and ready in less time than it would take to get one delivered! I'm fortunate to work with some amazing Indian chefs, and this is my adaption of one of their most popular recipes.

Serves 4

200g basmati rice

40g unsalted butter

1 tablespoon vegetable oil

1 onion, finely sliced

50g medium curry paste

4 small chicken breasts, cut into 2cm
   thick slices

200g tinned chopped tomatoes

300ml coconut milk

2 tablespoons roughly chopped
   coriander leaves

2 tablespoons roughly chopped
   mint leaves

1 lime, juiced

sea salt and freshly ground black pepper

3 tablespoons desiccated coconut,
   lightly toasted

Place the basmati rice in a medium saucepan, then pour on 400ml of cold water and add a knob of butter. Cover with a lid, then set over a high heat and bring to a simmer. Reduce the heat to low and cook for 12–15 minutes, while you make the curry.

Heat a large sauté pan or wok until hot. Add the vegetable oil and onion, and stir-fry for 2–3 minutes, until just softening, then add the curry paste and stir-fry for 1 minute. Add the chicken and stir to coat in the sauce, then add the tomatoes and coconut milk, and bring to the boil. Reduce the heat and simmer for 10 minutes until the chicken is cooked through and the sauce has thickened slightly. Stir in the chopped coriander and mint, then add the lime juice and the rest of the butter, and season to taste with salt and pepper.

The rice should be cooked by now – lift the lid and see if all the water has been absorbed. The rice should have little pockmarks all over it and be light and fluffy, in separate grains.

Serve the rice with a ladleful of chicken curry and the toasted desiccated coconut.

Flageolet bean and bacon salad

When you want a meal that's ready in just 10 minutes, tinned beans and other pulses are great to have in your cupboard. Either hot or cold, they can form the main part of a simple and very quick dish like this. Buy good-quality ones, though, as some are in a strong brine that doesn't taste very nice. A nice dressing is the key.

Serves 4

1 tablespoon rapeseed oil

8 slices of smoked streaky bacon

2 tablespoons cider vinegar

1 shallot, finely sliced

400g tin flageolet beans, drained and rinsed

1 teaspoon truffle oil

3 tablespoons vegetable oil

sea salt and freshly ground black pepper

50g rocket leaves

1 head of romaine lettuce, roughly chopped

40g Parmesan cheese, broken into small nuggets

Heat a frying pan until hot. Add the rapeseed oil and bacon, and fry on each side for a couple of minutes until golden-brown and crispy. Drain on kitchen paper, then roughly chop.

Return the frying pan to the heat, then add the cider vinegar and deglaze the pan, scraping up all the meaty bits from the bottom of the pan. Add the shallot and flageolet beans, and warm through.

Mix the truffle oil and vegetable oil together in a bowl, then add the flageolet bean mixture and toss to coat in the dressing. Season with pepper and a touch of salt to taste.

Divide the rocket and romaine lettuce between your serving plates and spoon the beans over the top, finishing with a scattering of Parmesan nuggets.

Artichoke and broad bean risotto

My artichoke plants have been in the garden some eight years now, and still produce a great crop year on year. If you can, try to get the smaller artichokes for this recipe, as they're easier to prepare and cook. The little bit of lemon at the end makes all the difference to this dish.

Serves 4

1 lemon
6 baby purple artichokes
200ml extra virgin olive oil
25g unsalted butter
2 shallots, finely chopped
1 garlic clove, finely chopped
3 sprigs of fresh thyme, leaves only
100g risotto rice
200ml white wine
750ml hot chicken or vegetable stock
150g podded broad beans, inner skins removed
4 heaped tablespoons grated Parmesan cheese, plus extra to serve
2 tablespoons finely chopped chives
50ml double cream
salt and freshly ground black pepper
1 chive flower, to garnish

Remove the zest from half the lemon and set aside. Cut the lemon in half. Peel the stalk of one artichoke, then trim to about 2.5cm below the base and remove the tough outer leaves. Cut the top third off and discard, then rub immediately with the halved lemon. Repeat with the rest of the artichokes.

Put 200ml of water into a sauté pan, then add the olive oil and bring to a simmer. Cut the artichokes in half lengthways, then add to the pan, cover with a lid and simmer for 10–15 minutes until tender. Check with the tip of a knife to see if they are cooked through – there should be no resistance. Remove from the heat and cool slightly, then cut in half lengthways.

Heat a sauté pan until medium hot. Add a knob of the butter, the shallots, garlic and thyme, and cook for a couple of minutes without colouring. Tip in the rice and stir well, then add the wine and cook until reduced to nothing.

Add a ladleful of hot stock and bring to a simmer, stirring occasionally, until the rice has absorbed it all. Keep adding stock a ladleful at a time, waiting until it has been absorbed before adding more. After you've been adding the stock for 5–6 minutes, add the broad beans and continue adding the stock until it has been used and the rice is tender – it should take 12–15 minutes.

When the rice is cooked through, add the artichokes, Parmesan, chives, lemon zest and cream, and season with salt and pepper to taste. Add a little more stock if needed to keep the risotto loose.

Serve with extra Parmesan grated over the top and the chive flower.

Sharing Comforts

Chicken and chorizo broth

A fantastic quick and simple meal that you can knock up in less than 10 minutes. The key is its strong flavours from the rosemary, thyme and a little bit of sage, which really bulk up the flavour of the beans.

Serves 6–8

4 tablespoons olive oil

1 onion, finely chopped

125g chorizo picante, finely chopped

6 boneless skinless chicken thighs, roughly chopped

½ teaspoon smoked hot paprika

5 garlic cloves, finely chopped

2 sprigs of rosemary, leaves picked and finely chopped

2 x 400g tins flageolet beans, drained and rinsed

800ml chicken stock

150ml double cream

50g unsalted butter

1 small bunch of flat-leaf parsley, roughly chopped

sea salt and freshly ground black pepper

500g sliced wheat and rye bread

Heat a large sauté pan until hot, then add half the olive oil, the onion and chorizo, and cook for 2 minutes. Add the chicken and fry for a couple of minutes, then add the smoked paprika, garlic and rosemary, and stir in the beans.

Add the stock, cream and butter, and bring to the boil, then simmer for 5 minutes until the chicken is cooked through. Add the parsley and season to taste with salt and pepper.

Heat a griddle pan until hot, then drizzle the bread with the last of the olive oil and griddle on each side until charred.

Serve the bread with the soup.

Braised hogget pie

Wherever possible and whenever the season allows, I always try to buy hogget or mutton. Hogget is a sheep that is between one and two years of age, and it has a much deeper and more intense flavour than young lamb. It lends itself well to this kind of braising or slow cooking to make it nice and tender.

Serves 6–8

1.5kg boneless shoulder of hogget
sea salt and freshly ground black pepper
6 shallots, thickly sliced
2 tablespoons tomato purée
2 garlic cloves, crushed
4 carrots, cut into large dice
2 celery sticks, thickly sliced
1 small bunch of thyme
1 bottle of red wine
500ml beef stock
1kg waxy potatoes, peeled and thickly sliced
50g butter

Preheat the oven to 200°C/400°F/gas mark 6.

Season the hogget well with salt and pepper. Heat a large casserole dish until hot, then add the hogget and seal on each side until browned. Remove and set aside. Add the shallots and tomato purée, and cook for a couple of minutes. Add the garlic, carrots and celery, and sweat for a few minutes.

Place the hogget on top and add the thyme and red wine. Bring to the boil, add the stock, return to a simmer, then place in the oven and cook for 2 hours.

Lift the hogget out of the dish and set on a board to cool slightly. Adjust the seasoning of the sauce, then tear the meat into strips and return them to the pan, mixing them well with the sauce and vegetables.

Layer the sliced potatoes over the meat in the casserole dish, then dot over the butter and season with salt and pepper. Return to the oven and cook for another 30 minutes until hot, golden and bubbling.

Aubergine and lentil lasagne

I'm a massive fan of moussaka and lasagne. So often vegetarian food can be a bit boring, but it doesn't need to be that way, as ingredients like aubergine and lentils can taste amazing when cooked properly.

Serves 4–6

For the filling

3 tablespoons olive oil
1 onion, roughly chopped
2 garlic cloves, finely chopped
2 aubergines, roughly chopped
1 tablespoon tomato purée
200g Puy lentils, rinsed
3 sprigs of thyme, leaves picked
150ml white wine
400g tin chopped tomatoes
500ml vegetable stock
sea salt and freshly ground black pepper
9 lasagne sheets

For the white sauce

25g unsalted butter
25g plain flour
500ml milk
275g Cheddar cheese, grated
a pinch of freshly grated nutmeg

Preheat the oven to 200°C/400°F/gas mark 6.

Heat a large sauté pan until hot. Add the olive oil, onion and garlic, and sweat gently for 5 minutes until softened. Turn the heat up, add the aubergines and fry until just golden.

Add the tomato purée and cook for 1 minute, then add the Puy lentils, thyme and white wine, stirring well. Add the tinned tomatoes and stock, and bring to the boil, then turn the heat down, cover and simmer for 30 minutes until the lentils are tender and the mixture has thickened. Season with salt and pepper, and set aside.

While the lentils cook, make the white sauce. Melt the butter in a saucepan, then whisk in the flour and cook for 1 minute. Whisk in the milk slowly, then continue to cook for 5 minutes, until thickened and silky smooth. Stir in 200g of the cheese and season with the nutmeg, salt and pepper.

Spoon one-third of the lentil mixture into the bottom of a medium ovenproof dish. Top with enough lasagne sheets to cover, then spoon over one-third of the white sauce. Repeat the layers of lentils, pasta and sauce until all have been used.

Top with the last of the cheese and then bake for 30 minutes, until golden brown and bubbling.

Ham hock and pumpkin risotto

I grow pumpkins in my garden – they have a fantastic flavour and produce amazing risotto. You can leave out the ham hock if you like, and just make the pumpkin risotto on its own; to change the flavour slightly, crush some amaretti biscuits over the top – pumpkin and almonds go together really well. See page 92 for one way to use up any leftover ham hock.

Serves 4

For the ham

1kg ham hock
1 onion, cut into chunks
2 bay leaves
4 sprigs of flat-leaf parsley
½ teaspoon black peppercorns
1 cinnamon stick, broken in half

For the pumpkin risotto

300g pumpkin, peeled and cut into
   large chunks
50g unsalted butter
1 onion, finely chopped
1 garlic clove, finely chopped
200g risotto rice
150ml dry white wine
1 litre of the ham stock (see method)
2 tablespoons mascarpone
25g Parmesan cheese, freshly grated
sea salt and freshly ground
   black pepper
2 tablespoons pea shoots

Place the ham hock, onion, bay leaves, parsley, peppercorns and cinnamon in a large saucepan, then top with cold water, so that the ham is covered. Bring to the boil, then turn down to a simmer and cook for 1½ hours. Remove from the heat and allow the ham to cool in the liquid.

Preheat the oven to 200°C/400°F/gas mark 6.

Place the pumpkin on a roasting tray in the oven and cook for 25–30 minutes, until soft. Place in a food processor and blitz to a purée, then set aside.

Meanwhile, heat a sauté pan until hot, add the butter, onion and garlic, and sweat for 2 minutes. Add the risotto rice and fry for 1 minute, stirring well, then add the wine and reduce to nothing. Gradually add the ham stock, a ladleful at a time, stirring well. Continue to add the stock until the rice is tender.

Add the puréed pumpkin, mascarpone and Parmesan, and stir well. Season with salt and pepper.

Spoon the risotto onto plates and shake gently to settle. Shred some of the ham hock and stack in the centre of the risotto. Top with a little pile of pea shoots.

Goat tagine with toasted nut couscous

I first tasted goat in France, but it's a staple meat in many countries in Africa, Asia and the Middle East. It has a similar taste to mutton, and it's delicious. Toasting the couscous in nut-brown butter enhances its natural flavour.

To make the tagine, put the cumin, turmeric, ras el hanout and saffron into a bowl with 2 tablespoons of the vegetable oil and mix well. Add the goat and toss to combine, then set aside.

Heat a large casserole dish until hot. Add the rest of the vegetable oil, the onion, garlic, ginger and chilli, and fry for 2–3 minutes until just softening. Add the meat and fry for a couple of minutes. Add the ginger, cinnamon stick, tinned tomatoes and honey, and mix well. Add 200ml of water and bring to the boil, then stir in the apricots and preserved lemon. Lower the heat and simmer for 45–60 minutes until the meat is tender and the sauce has thickened.

Check the seasoning, then stir in the chopped pistachios, mint, coriander and parsley.

To make the couscous, heat a frying pan until hot. Add the butter and when it's foaming, add the couscous and stir-fry until golden all over. Add 400ml of just-boiled water, mix well, then remove from the heat, cover with clingfilm and set aside to steam for 5 minutes.

Remove the clingfilm, stir with a fork to loosen the grains, then cover once more and leave for another 5 minutes. Stir in the nuts, apricots, preserved lemon, herbs and lemon juice and season well with salt and pepper.

To serve, pile the couscous into one serving bowl and ladle the tagine into another.

Serves 4

For the tagine

2 teaspoons ground cumin
1 teaspoon ground turmeric
2 teaspoons ras el hanout
½ teaspoon saffron strands
4 tablespoons vegetable oil
600g goat shoulder, neck and leg meat, cut into large dice
1 onion, diced
2 garlic cloves, chopped
4cm piece of ginger, unpeeled, finely grated
1 red chilli, chopped
1 cinnamon stick
400g tin chopped tomatoes
1 tablespoon honey
125g dried apricots, roughly chopped
1 medium preserved lemon, roughly chopped
sea salt and freshly ground black pepper
50g pistachio nuts, roughly chopped
3 tablespoons roughly chopped mint leaves
3 tablespoons roughly chopped coriander leaves
3 tablespoons roughly chopped flat-leaf parsley

For the couscous

25g unsalted butter
200g couscous
50g pistachio nuts, roughly chopped
50g flaked toasted almonds
50g toasted pine nuts
50g dried apricots, roughly chopped
1 preserved lemon, finely chopped
3 tablespoons roughly chopped mint leaves
3 tablespoon roughly chopped coriander stalks and leaves
3 tablespoons roughly chopped flat-leaf parsley
1 lemon, juiced

Roast chicken with asparagus fricassée into next-day chicken and asparagus quiche

Real men eat quiche. Or that is what the cameramen said as they dived into it when I cooked it on the show. Make this delicious roast chicken dinner and then use up the leftovers in the quiche the next day. Always serve the quiche at room temperature – never straight from the fridge. Cold quiche reminds me of terrible wedding food.

Serves 4–6

For the roast chicken

1 onion, roughly chopped
2 carrots, roughly chopped
1 x 1.5kg whole chicken
sea salt and freshly ground black pepper
2 tablespoons rapeseed oil
75g unsalted butter
150g asparagus, cut into 3cm long pieces
100g fresh peas, podded
1 tablespoon marjoram leaves
1 shallot, finely sliced into rings

For the chicken and asparagus quiche

unsalted butter, for greasing
300g ready-made shortcrust pastry
plain flour, for dusting
8 eggs, plus 1 beaten egg for eggwash
600ml double cream
300g cooked chicken, cut into 3cm chunks
100g asparagus
100g vintage Comté cheese, finely grated
1 bag of salad leaves

For the roast chicken, preheat the oven to 200°C/400°F/gas mark 6.

Put the onion and carrots into a deep-sided roasting tray, then place the chicken on top. Season with salt and pepper, and add a drizzle of rapeseed oil, then add 75ml of water to the tray. Roast for 1–1¼ hours until cooked through. To check if the chicken is cooked, pierce the thickest part of the thigh with a skewer or knife – if the juices run clear the chicken is cooked; if not, return it to the oven for a further 10 minutes, then check again. Remove from the oven and let it rest for 10 minutes before carving.

While the chicken rests, make the fricassée. Heat a frying pan until hot, and add half the butter and 200ml of water. Bring to a simmer, then add the asparagus, peas, marjoram and shallot, and return to a simmer. Cook for 3–4 minutes, until the vegetables are tender, then whisk in the remaining butter and season with salt and pepper.

Carve half the chicken into slices and serve with the fricassée.

The next day, to make the chicken and asparagus quiche, preheat the oven to 200°C/400°F/gas mark 6 and butter a 23cm wide and 4cm deep loose-bottomed tart tin. Roll out the pastry on a lightly floured work surface, then lay it over the tin and press gently into the base and side. Line with several sheets of clingfilm and fill with flour or raw rice and bake for 20–25 minutes. Remove the clingfilm and filling, brush the inside of the tart with the beaten egg, then cook for 5 minutes, until golden.

Meanwhile, strip the remainder of the chicken meat and cut into 3cm chunks – you will need about 300g. Whisk the 8 eggs and cream together, then season with salt and pepper and set aside.

Reduce the oven to 180°C/350°F/gas mark 4. Lay the asparagus in the pastry base, then put the chicken and marjoram on top. Pull the oven rack out slightly and set the quiche near the edge. Pour over the egg mixture, then scatter with the Comté. Slide the quiche fully into the oven and bake for 20–25 minutes, until just set and golden. Cool slightly, then serve with the salad.

Shellfish cassoulet

You can make this with a mixture of any shellfish, and you can include oily fish or fresh tuna. If you're adding shellfish like mussels and clams, add them in the last 5 minutes to avoid overcooking. I cook this in a wood-fired pizza oven, but any heavy-based pot in a hot oven will do fine. You can even make it on a barbecue with a lid, which gives it an added smokiness. The combination of bread, fish and tomatoes tastes superb.

Serves 4

1 onion, roughly chopped
6 garlic cloves, crushed
200ml extra virgin olive oil
1 head of fennel, roughly chopped
1 teaspoon fennel seeds
4 star anise
300ml white wine
2 x 400g tins chopped tomatoes
a handful of torn basil leaves
200g puréed brown crabmeat
1 small sourdough loaf, cut into
  small chunks
1 cooked small lobster, cut into pieces
3 x 75g cod or pollock fillets, skin on
1 mackerel, cut into large chunks
12 raw tiger prawns, shells on
1kg mussels
freshly ground black pepper

Preheat the oven to as high as it will go.

Put the onion, garlic, 75ml of the olive oil, the fennel, fennel seeds, star anise and half the white wine into a large ovenproof sauté pan. Stir well, then place in the oven for 5–6 minutes until just softened. Remove and stir well, then mix in the tomatoes, half the basil and the crabmeat, and return to the oven for another 5 minutes.

Meanwhile, put the chunks of bread into a roasting tray, drizzle with 50ml of the olive oil, toss to coat, then take the sauce out of the oven and put the bread in to roast for a few minutes until just browned.

Add the lobster, cod or pollock, mackerel, prawns, mussels and the rest of the wine to the pan of sauce, then add lots of black pepper. Return to the oven for 8–10 minutes, or until the fish is cooked through.

Scatter the croutons on top of the fish, then sprinkle the remainder of the basil over the top, and finish with the last of the olive oil.

Serve in the cooking pot at the table.

Cooking on a beer can is nothing new: in Australia they've been doing it for years. The secret is that the beer keeps the inside of the chicken nice and moist while it's cooking on the barbecue. You'll need a barbecue with a lid, and you can cook the jacket potatoes in foil alongside. With added garlic butter at the end, this makes a truly delicious summertime meal.

Beer can piri piri chicken with garlic butter jacket potatoes

Serves 4

1½ tablespoons sweet smoked paprika

½ tablespoon hot smoked paprika

½ teaspoon chilli flakes

2 tablespoons Dijon mustard

1 tablespoon red wine vinegar

3 limes

3 lemons

5 tablespoons olive oil, plus extra to drizzle

1 x 2kg whole chicken

4 baking potatoes, scrubbed

sea salt and freshly ground black pepper

2 garlic bulbs

1 can of beer, half full

3 tablespoons finely chopped chives

250g unsalted butter, softened

1 head of lettuce, root removed and leaves separated

4 ripe tomatoes, cut into chunks

¼ cucumber, cut in half lengthways, then into slices

2 tablespoons extra virgin olive oil

Put both the paprikas, chilli flakes, Dijon mustard, red wine vinegar, the juice of 1 lime and of 1 lemon into a bowl and mix to a paste. Pour the paste into a large plastic bag, then add the olive oil and the chicken. Seal at the end and shake around so that the chicken is covered in spices.

Prick the potatoes, then rub with a little oil, salt and black pepper, and wrap each one in foil. Place 1 garlic bulb on another sheet of foil and drizzle with oil, then twist tight.

Cut the second garlic bulb in half and place inside the chicken, then manoeuvre the half-full beer can into the bottom of the chicken too. The beer will bubble up and create steam inside the chicken, keeping it moist as it cooks, but you only need the can to be half full otherwise it will spill over.

Put the potatoes and garlic on a barbecue, then place the chicken upright, standing on the beer can in the centre. Make a silver foil collar for the base of the chicken to protect it slightly, then cover with a lid and roast for 15 minutes. Remove the garlic bulb and roast for another 30 minutes, until the chicken is cooked through and the potatoes are tender. If you want to cook this in a roasting tray in the oven, you will probably need to place the chicken on a low shelf to fit it in. Cook the garlic for 15 minutes and the chicken and potatoes for 45–60 minutes, at 200°C/400°F/gas mark 6.

Take the cooked garlic out of the foil and allow to cool. Cut the top off the bulb and squeeze the cooked garlic out into a bowl. Add the chives and the softened butter, and mix together.

Toss the lettuce, tomatoes and cucumber together in a large serving bowl, and drizzle with a little extra virgin olive oil. Cut the remaining limes and lemons into chunks.

Place the cooked chicken on the beer can in the centre of a serving platter. Loosen the foil from the potatoes, cut a cross in the top of them, squeeze gently and spoon the garlic butter on top. Place them around the chicken and garnish with the lemons and limes.

'Nduja and sheep's cheese pizza

'Nduja is one of the ingredients I came across while working with another chef, Francesco Mazzi. It comes from, Calabria, his region of Italy. It's a wonderful spicy – and I mean spicy – soft sausage that contains so much flavour. I love it with gnocchi, but on this pizza, made in my oven in the garden, it tastes amazing.

Serves 6

For the pizza dough

200g semolina flour

800g '00' white flour, plus extra for dusting

1 tablespoon caster sugar

1 teaspoon salt

7g fresh yeast

650ml warm water

For the topping

400g tin San Marzano tomatoes

400g sheep's cheese, sliced and crumbled

300g 'nduja (soft spicy salami from Calabria, Italy)

a large handful of basil leaves

1 tablespoon peanut oil

Place the flours, sugar and salt in a large bowl, and stir. Mix the yeast to a paste with a little of the warm water, then pour onto the flour. Add the rest of the water, gradually mixing in the flour to form a soft dough.

Tip the dough out onto a lightly floured work surface and knead until smooth and elastic. Place in a bowl and leave to rise for 1½ hours, then knock back and divide into six equal portions. Roll each piece into a ball, then place on a tray, cover and leave to rise for 4 hours or overnight in the fridge.

Preheat the oven to as high as it will go. Place a heavy baking tray or pizza stone in the oven to heat up.

Roll each piece of dough out on a lightly floured surface, until about 5mm thick, then place on an upturned floured tray.

Place the tomatoes in a food processor and blitz to a purée. Spoon the tomato purée thinly over the bases, just to the edges. Scatter over the sheep's cheese, 'nduja and basil leaves, and drizzle over the peanut oil.

Scoot into the oven, pushing the pizza onto the heated baking tray or pizza stone, and cook for 5–8 minutes until cooked through and bubbling. You will need to cook the pizzas in batches. Serve immediately.

Classic coq au vin – à la Floyd

This classic French dish – made here in honour of the legend Keith Floyd – traditionally uses wine from Burgundy. However, many regions of France have a version made with their own local wine – from coq au Riesling in Alsace to coq au violet, using beaujolais nouveau wine. There is even a coq au Champagne. Serve the rich chicken and lardons with just some simple, creamy, buttery mashed potatoes.

Serves 4–6

2kg good-quality chicken, cut into 10 pieces

1 teaspoon plain flour

175g unsalted butter

1 onion, roughly chopped

225g smoked streaky bacon, cut into lardons

500ml red wine

50ml brandy

2 garlic cloves, lightly crushed

3 bay leaves

4 sprigs of thyme

1kg King Edward potatoes, peeled and cut into chunks

sea salt and freshly ground black pepper

200ml double cream

100g silverskin onions

200g baby button mushrooms

Sprinkle the chicken pieces with the flour and toss to coat thoroughly. Heat a large casserole dish until hot and add 50g of the butter. When it's foaming, add the chicken in batches, skin-side down, and cook until brown on each side. Remove from the pan, then add the onion and fry for 1–2 minutes.

Return the chicken to the casserole, then add the bacon and fry for 1 minute. Add the red wine, brandy, garlic, bay leaves and thyme, and bring to the boil. Reduce the heat and simmer for 1 hour until the chicken is cooked through.

While the chicken cooks, make the mash. Place the potatoes in a pan of cold, salted water and bring to the boil, then reduce the heat and simmer for 12–15 minutes, or until the potatoes are tender. Drain and return to the pan, then place over a low heat for a couple of minutes to dry the potatoes slightly.

Pass the potatoes through a ricer, then beat in 100g of the butter and the double cream to form a very smooth mash. Season to taste with salt and pepper.

When the chicken is cooked, heat a frying pan until hot and add the remaining butter. When it's foaming, add the silverskin onions and button mushrooms, and cook until golden. Add them to the chicken, stir through and season to taste.

Serve the coq au vin with a dollop of mash.

Spiced quinoa, cauliflower, pine nut and blue cheese salad

Quinoa – one of the great superfoods – is a type of seed originating from Peru. It comes from the same family as beetroot, spinach and tumbleweed, and is really high in protein, making it popular in vegetarian cooking. Once you've tried it you will appreciate its unique texture and flavour.

Serves 4

70g quinoa
2 tablespoons olive oil
½ small cauliflower, cut into florets, then into thick slices
4 shallots, finely chopped
1 teaspoon medium curry powder
4 tablespoons red wine vinegar
100ml maple syrup
4 tablespoons extra virgin olive oil
sea salt and freshly ground black pepper
4 heads of baby gem lettuce, cut into quarters
50g pine nuts
2 tablespoons finely chopped chives
150g Gorgonzola dolce or soft blue cheese

Cook the quinoa according to the packet instructions, then drain and set aside.

Meanwhile, heat a frying pan until hot. Add 1 tablespoon of the olive oil and the cauliflower florets, and cook until lightly browned on each side, then remove and place in a large bowl.

Add the rest of the olive oil to the frying pan with the shallots and fry for a couple of minutes until just softened, then add the curry powder and cook for 2 more minutes, stirring well.

Add the red wine vinegar and turn the heat down to a simmer the dressing, then stir in the maple syrup and olive oil. Simmer for 1 minute, then remove from the heat.

Pour half the dressing into the cooked drained quinoa, season with salt and pepper, and toss well so that it is coated thoroughly. Pour the remaining dressing into the bowl with the cooked cauliflower, add the baby gems, pine nuts and half the chives, season and toss together. Add the dressed quinoa and toss lightly together, then divide between four plates. Place the small pieces of blue cheese over the salad, finish with a scattering of chives and serve straight away.

Lamb belly with bbq sauce and pickled red onions

While filming TV shows and on my travels I've found that there are ingredients that are a bit harder to get hold of. Lamb belly is one such cut of meat, but it's worth seeking out. You can order it in advance from a butcher; it's inexpensive and makes for one of the tastiest dishes in this book. You can also add a quarter of a cucumber, finely sliced, to the red onion pickle to give it a fresher crunch.

Serves 4–6

For the lamb

1 carrot, roughly chopped
1 onion, roughly chopped
2 star anise
1 head of garlic, cut in half
1 small bunch of parsley
1 dried smoked chipotle chilli
1 x 1.75kg lamb belly, bones removed

For the pickled red onions

2 red onions, finely sliced
200ml cider vinegar
2 tablespoons caster sugar
½ teaspoon black mustard seeds
½ teaspoon sea salt

For the barbecue sauce

75g chipotle paste
275ml tomato ketchup
175ml maple syrup
1 tablespoon Worcestershire sauce
1 tablespoon cider vinegar
75ml light soy sauce

To serve

8–12 pitta breads or pides
1 small bunch of coriander

Put the carrot, onion, star anise, garlic, parsley and chipotle chilli into a large saucepan, half fill with cold water, then lay the lamb belly on top and pour over more water if necessary, to cover. Bring to the boil, then turn the heat down and simmer for 1 hour, until really tender. Drain and place on a board until cool enough to handle.

Preheat the oven to 200°C/400°F/gas mark 6.

While the lamb cooks, pickle the red onions. Put the sliced red onions into a bowl, then heat the cider vinegar, caster sugar, mustard seeds and salt until just simmering and the sugar has dissolved. Pour over the onions, stir well and leave to cool.

Meanwhile, make the barbecue sauce. Heat a frying pan until hot, add the chipotle paste and fry for a couple of minutes, then add the ketchup and maple syrup, and cook for 2–3 minutes until it's bubbling up. Add the Worcestershire sauce, cider vinegar and soy sauce, bring to the boil, then reduce the heat and simmer for 5–6 minutes until thickened.

Put the naan bread or pides into the oven for a few minutes to warm through.

Shred the lamb into thick pieces and fold them into the warm barbecue sauce. Serve the lamb on top of the hot bread, with the pickled red onions and coriander leaves scattered over the top.

Piperade is a mixture of onions, peppers and tomatoes, with the addition of espelette pepper. The dish originates from the Basque region, on the French/Spanish border. The espelette pepper is traditional in the northern part of the region and can be bought dried, puréed or pickled in jars, but most commonly it's found as ground pepper. Once the veg are cooked you can add egg, garlic or a meat such as ham, but I love it with chicken and simply cooked pilau rice. It's also a dish that gets better the second time you cook it.

Chicken piperade with pilau rice

Serves 4–6

For the chicken

1 x 1.5kg chicken, giblets removed, cut into 8 pieces

1 tablespoon plain flour

sea salt and freshly ground black pepper

25ml olive oil

2 onions, thickly sliced

2 garlic cloves, lightly crushed

4 red peppers, seeded and thickly sliced

1 tablespoon tomato purée

75ml dry sherry

75ml white wine

400g tin chopped tomatoes

2 teaspoons ground espelette pepper

1–2 teaspoons caster sugar, to taste

2 tablespoons finely chopped flat-leaf parsley

For the rice

2 tablespoons vegetable oil

1 onion, finely diced

6 cloves

1 cinnamon stick

200g basmati rice

2 bay leaves

1 lemon

Preheat the oven to 180°C/350°F/gas mark 4.

Heat a large sauté pan until hot. Dust the chicken pieces with the flour and season with salt and pepper. Heat a little of the olive oil in a sauté pan and seal the chicken on each side, in batches, until golden-brown. Remove from the pan and place in an ovenproof casserole.

Add the rest of the olive oil to the sauté pan, then add the onions, garlic and peppers, and cook for 5 minutes until just softening. Add the tomato purée and sauté for 1 minute, then add the sherry and white wine, and bring to a simmer.

Add the tinned tomatoes, espelette pepper and sugar, and stir well to combine, then pour over the chicken. Cover with a lid and bake for 1–1½ hours, until the chicken is cooked through, the peppers are tender and the sauce has reduced slightly.

While the chicken cooks, make the rice. Heat a wide sauté pan until hot, then add the oil and onion and sweat for 2 minutes. Add the cloves and cinnamon, and cook for another minute.

Add the rice and stir well to combine, coating all the grains in the onion mixture, then add 600ml water and stir once more. Add the bay leaves and 2 slices of the lemon, then cover with a lid and reduce to a gentle simmer. Cook for 15–20 minutes until the rice is tender and all the liquid is absorbed. Taste and add the rest of the lemon if necessary.

Season the chicken to taste with salt and pepper, then stir in the parsley. Serve with the pilau rice.

Beef and carrot pie

Who doesn't like a pie? The combination of beef and carrots here is a truly great classic pairing. And as the carrots are lovely and chunky, they won't disintegrate as they cook with the beef.

Serves 4–6

For the filling

1kg stewing steak, kept in large pieces
2 tablespoons plain flour
sea salt and freshly ground black pepper
2 tablespoons rapeseed oil
2 onions, thickly sliced
200ml ale
400ml beef stock
300g Chantenay carrots, cleaned
2 egg yolks, lightly beaten

For the pastry

250g plain flour, plus extra for dusting
150g cold unsalted butter, diced
1 teaspoon fine sea salt
1 egg

Toss the beef and flour together in a bowl, and season with salt and pepper. Heat a large casserole dish until hot, then add half the rapeseed oil and enough of the beef to just cover the bottom of the casserole. Fry until browned on each side, then remove and set aside. Repeat with the remaining oil and beef in batches.

Add the onions and fry for 2–3 minutes until just softened, then return the beef to the pan. Add the ale and beef stock, and bring to the boil, season with salt and pepper, then turn down to a simmer and cook for 1½ hours until the beef is just tender.

Stir the carrots into the pan and simmer for another 30 minutes, until the beef and carrots are tender. Check the seasoning and set aside to cool.

While the beef is cooking, make the pastry. Place the flour in a bowl, add the butter and salt, and rub between your fingertips until the mixture looks a little like coarse breadcrumbs.

Make a well in the centre and crack in the egg. Using the tips of your fingers, mix until a sticky dough forms. Tip out onto a floured work surface and knead lightly until smooth. Flatten to about 1cm thick, then cover with clingfilm and place in the fridge to rest for at least 30 minutes.

When the beef is cold, preheat the oven to 200°C/400°F/gas mark 6.

Spoon the beef into a large pie dish (or, if your casserole dish is shallow enough, keep the beef in its cooking pan). Roll out the pastry on a floured work surface to 5mm thick. Brush the edges of the dish with the beaten egg yolks and lay the pastry over the top.

Cut around the edge, so there is just enough pastry to crimp at the edges, and brush with the remaining egg. Bake for 30–40 minutes, until the pastry is golden and cooked through.

Dahl chicken, chilli paneer and naan

I'm fortunate to count some top Indian chefs among my mates and I cooked this dish with Cyrus Todiwala on the show who is not only a true gentleman but also a hugely talented cook. Thanks for the advice and tips – I think it's one of my favourite recipes in the book!

Start with the naan. Place the flour in a food mixer fitted with a dough hook, or a large bowl, with the yeast and baking powder, and add the egg, sugar and salt. Mix together, then add the yoghurt and milk, and mix to a soft dough. Set aside to rise for 1 hour, then knead briefly until smooth and divide into six equal balls. Cover and set aside to rise in a warm place for another hour.

To make the dahl, rinse the lentils and soak them in 500ml water for 20 minutes.

Heat a large sauté pan until hot. Add half the oil and the dried chillies, and fry for 1 minute, then add the green chillies and onions, and sauté for 3–4 minutes until lightly coloured. Add the curry leaves, ginger, and garlic and continue to fry.

Mix the chilli powder, ground cumin, coriander and turmeric together in a small bowl with 150ml of the chicken stock to form a paste. Add to the pan and cook until you see the oil separate out – another 2–3 minutes. Add the lentils and their soaking water, and bring to the boil, then add the salt, cover with a lid and simmer for 5 minutes. Add the butter, cover, and simmer while you cook the chicken.

Chop the chicken into chunks. Heat a separate sauté pan until hot, add the rest of the oil and the chicken, and sauté for 3–4 minutes until coloured and nearly cooked.

Add the lentils to the chicken along with the tinned tomatoes and the rest of the chicken stock. Cook for another 15–20 minutes until the chicken is cooked through and

the lentils are tender. Stir in the tamarind, brown sugar, coriander and mint, and check the seasoning. Add a little more stock if it becomes too thick. Leave to simmer gently on a very low heat.

While the chicken is cooking, make the chilli paneer. Cut the paneer into strips about 1cm wide and 3cm long. Heat a wok until hot, then add enough oil to cover the base by 2.5cm. Heat until shimmering, then fry the paneer in batches until golden brown. Drain into a sieve set over a bowl.

Discard the majority of the oil, leaving enough to just coat the bottom of the wok. Add the pine nuts, chillies, ginger and garlic, and stir-fry for 2 minutes. Add the red onion and both peppers, and stir-fry for 2 minutes, then add the vinegar, soy sauce and chicken stock, and bring to a simmer. Add the spring onions and simmer for 1 minute. Mix the cornflour with 3 tablespoons of cold water to make a paste, then whisk into the peppers and onion, and cook until just thickened. Stir in the paneer and leave to simmer on a very low heat.

To cook the naan, preheat the oven as high as it will go. Place a heavy baking tray or pizza stone in the oven and allow to heat. Stretch the dough to an oval shape, then place on the tray or stone and bake for 4–5 minutes, until risen and golden brown. Brush with the melted butter.

Finish the chilli paneer with the coriander, and serve with the dahl chicken and naan.

Serves 4

For the dahl chicken

250g red lentils
4 tablespoons vegetable oil
2 dried red chillies, torn, seeds removed
2 long green chillies, finely chopped
2 onions, finely chopped
1 tablespoon chopped curry leaves
5cm piece of ginger, peeled, finely chopped
6 garlic cloves, finely chopped
1 teaspoon hot red chilli powder
1 teaspoon ground cumin
2 teaspoons ground coriander
1 teaspoon turmeric
300ml chicken stock
1 teaspoon sea salt
40g unsalted butter
6 boneless skinless chicken thighs
200g tinned chopped tomatoes
1 tablespoon tamarind paste
1 tablespoon dark brown soft sugar
1 small bunch of coriander, chopped
2 tablespoons chopped mint leaves

For the chilli paneer

450g paneer
vegetable oil, for shallow-frying
50g pine nuts
4 long green finger chillies, finely sliced
5cm piece of ginger, peeled, finely chopped
8 garlic cloves, finely chopped
1 red onion, finely sliced
1 green pepper, finely sliced
1 long red pepper, finely sliced
50ml white wine vinegar
75ml light soy sauce
250ml chicken stock
3 spring onions, finely sliced
1 tablespoon cornflour
2 tablespoons chopped coriander

For the naan

450g plain flour
2 teaspoons fast-action dried yeast
1 teaspoon baking powder
1 egg
1 teaspoon caster sugar
a pinch of sea salt
150ml natural yoghurt
150ml milk
50g melted unsalted butter

This started off with me just wanting to make fish and chips, and it turned into something else. Let's face it, you can't have fish and chips without bread and butter, and homemade tartare sauce brings the whole thing together in one sandwich. A bit extravagant, I know, but my goodness, it tastes delicious.

Battered pollock, mushy pea and lemon mayo baguette

Serves 4–6

For the mushy peas

225g dried marrowfat peas
1 teaspoon bicarbonate of soda
25g unsalted butter
sea salt and freshly ground black pepper

For the pollock

200g plain flour
15g fresh yeast or 8g fast-action
  dried yeast
a pinch of caster sugar
a pinch of sea salt
1 tablespoon cider vinegar
300ml beer
vegetable oil and dripping, for deep-
  frying
1kg pollock fillets, skin on, pin-boned
  and cut into 5cm pieces

For the lemon mayonnaise

2 egg yolks
1 teaspoon English mustard
300ml rapeseed oil
2 lemons, zested and juiced

To serve

50g softened unsalted butter
1 long baguette, split horizontally

Soak the peas in a large bowl in three times their volume of water with the bicarbonate of soda, for at least 12 hours, preferably overnight.

Drain the peas, rinse under cold running water, then place on the stove in a large pan and cover with water. Cover and bring to the boil, then reduce the heat and simmer the peas for 20–30 minutes, stirring from time to time. They should be soft and mushy in texture, but not too dry. If they are wet, continue cooking them with the lid off to dry them out a little. Beat in the butter and season with salt and pepper.

To make the lemon mayo, place the egg yolks and mustard in a food processor, and blend until pale and creamy. With the motor running, pour in the oil in a slow, steady stream, until the mayonnaise is thick (you may not need all the oil). Mix in the lemon zest and juice, and season to taste.

To cook the pollock, mix the flour, yeast, sugar, salt and vinegar together in a bowl. Add the beer and whisk until the mixture forms a thick batter. Set aside to ferment for about 30 minutes – it is ready to use when the mixture starts to bubble.

Heat a deep-fat fryer to 190°C/375°F, or heat the oil for deep-frying in a deep heavy-based frying pan until a breadcrumb sizzles and turns brown when dropped into it. (CAUTION: Hot oil can be dangerous. Do not leave unattended.)

Dip each piece of fish into the batter to coat thoroughly. Lower carefully into the fryer and cook one at a time. Fry for 4–6 minutes, until the fish is cooked through and the batter is golden-brown. Scatter the remaining batter into the fat fryer and fry until golden-brown. Drain the fish on kitchen paper and season with salt.

To serve, spread the softened butter along the length of the baguette and top with the mushy peas. Place pieces of pollock all along the mushy peas and drizzle over the lemon mayonnaise. Add the batter scraps, then cover with the top of the baguette and gently press down. Serve in one long piece and carve at the table.

Grilled vegetable pan bagnat

When you're making this it all looks a bit weird, but it will come together when you actually serve it. The chargrilled veg are layered with cheese, and you can add salmon, tuna, ham – whatever you want. You can even buy the roasted veg if you don't want to make your own. It's best left to sit in the fridge for a couple of hours so that all the flavours are absorbed into the bread.

Serves 4

1 aubergine, cut into 5mm dice
1 red onion, thickly sliced
6 asparagus stems, trimmed and cut into 1cm pieces
3 tablespoons olive oil
sea salt and freshly ground black pepper
130g sunblushed tomatoes, drained, and 100ml of the oil reserved
50g toasted pine nuts
50g pecorino cheese, freshly grated
4 ciabatta rolls
a large handful of basil leaves
1 ball of mozzarella cheese, drained and thinly sliced

Preheat the oven to 180°C/350°F/gas mark 4.

Heat a griddle pan until very hot. Toss the aubergine, red onion and asparagus with 1 tablespoon of the olive oil, season with salt and pepper, then place on the griddle in batches and grill for 2–3 minutes, until just cooked through. Remove and set aside to cool.

Put the sunblushed tomatoes into a food processor or a pestle and mortar with the 100ml of olive oil from the jar, and blitz to a chunky purée. Add the pine nuts and pecorino, and pulse until combined but still slightly chunky. Season the pesto with pepper and a pinch of salt.

Cut off the top quarter from the rolls. Set these aside – they will be the lids. Scoop out all the bread from inside the rolls and keep for making breadcrumbs. Brush the inside of the rolls with the remaining olive oil and place on a tray in the oven for 8–10 minutes, to crisp up.

Spread some of the tomato pesto in the bottom of the rolls, then layer in some mozzarella and basil leaves.

Divide the griddled vegetables between the rolls, then top with more pesto, mozzarella and basil leaves. Place the lids on top and press down lightly.

This can be eaten immediately, or wrapped in clingfilm and kept in the fridge for up to 3 days, then either eaten cold or heated through in the oven preheated to 200°C/400°F/gas mark 6 for 15 minutes until hot through.

Tandoori chicken lollipop drumsticks with raita

The key to this in the preparation. Making the lollipops is simple enough, but you do need to get yourself some pliers and remove the tendons from the drumsticks, otherwise they are awkward to eat.

Using the heel of a heavy knife, chop through the top of each drumstick, taking the knuckle off. Turn upside down and chop the bottom of the bone off, then press the meat down towards the bottom of the bone so that it looks like a little ball at the bottom of the drumstick. Using a pair of tweezers, pull the tendons out and discard. Repeat with all the drumsticks, then set aside.

Place one-third of the yoghurt in a bowl with the remaining drumstick ingredients and mix to a paste, then mix in the rest of the yoghurt. Put the drumsticks into the marinade and wriggle them around so that they are coated properly. Cover and place in the fridge to marinate for at least 4 hours, preferably overnight.

Preheat the oven to 200°C/400°F/gas mark 6. Remove the drumsticks from the fridge and place on a baking tray, bones upright. Roast for 12–15 minutes until browned and cooked through.

While the drumsticks roast, make the raita. Put the chilli, garlic and cucumber in a bowl and mix together, then add the cumin, mint and coriander, and mix once more. Add the yoghurt and lime juice, season to taste with salt and pepper, then place in the fridge until the chicken is ready.

Pile the drumsticks onto a plate, spoon the raita into a bowl and serve the two together.

Serves 4

For the drumsticks

12 chicken drumsticks
300ml natural yoghurt
1 teaspoon garam masala
1 teaspoon ground cumin
1 tablespoon chilli powder
½ teaspoon ground turmeric
½ teaspoon ground cinnamon
5cm piece of ginger, unpeeled, finely grated
1 garlic clove, finely chopped
1 lemon, juiced

For the raita dip

1 green chilli, finely chopped
1 garlic clove, finely chopped
½ cucumber, finely diced
½ teaspoon ground cumin
2 tablespoons finely chopped mint leaves
2 tablespoons finely chopped coriander leaves
200ml natural yoghurt
1 lime, juiced
sea salt and freshly ground black pepper

Spiced pork and pomegranate tabbouleh

Many people think that tabbouleh is made with couscous, but for me it should always be made with bulghur wheat – a traditional Middle Eastern cracked grain. The spiced pork and pomegranate molasses go so well together, but you could also make this dish with chicken or fish.

Serves 4

1 large bunch of coriander, roughly chopped

1 large bunch of mint, roughly chopped

3 lemons, juiced

1 teaspoon ground coriander

1 teaspoon ground cumin

½ teaspoon sumac

2 tablespoons za'atar

150ml extra virgin olive oil

450g pork tenderloin, trimmed of sinew and thickly sliced

1 pomegranate, seeded

3 tomatoes, chopped

8 spring onions, roughly chopped

1 large bunch of flat-leaf parsley, roughly chopped

125g bulghur wheat, soaked in cold water for 2 hours, then drained

2 tablespoons pomegranate molasses

2 tablespoons clear honey

sea salt and freshly ground black pepper

50g flaked toasted almonds

Put a small handful of the chopped coriander and mint into a bowl with the juice of 1 of the lemons and the ground coriander, cumin, sumac and half the za'atar. Add 50ml of the olive oil and mix well. Add the pork and stir to coat, then set aside while you make the tabbouleh.

Put the pomegranate seeds, tomatoes, spring onions, all the remaining herbs and the soaked and drained bulghur wheat into a large bowl, and mix together.

Mix the remaining lemon juice, pomegranate molasses, honey and 50ml of the olive oil together in a separate bowl, and season well with salt and pepper. Add to the salad, season generously with more salt and pepper, then stir in the flaked almonds.

Heat a frying pan until hot, then add the last of the olive oil and the pork, and fry in batches for 2–3 minutes, until golden-brown and cooked through. Tip into a serving bowl with all the cooking oil, and serve with the tabbouleh.

Childhood Comforts

Cauliflower cheese with crispy maple syrup pancetta

To be honest, I wasn't sure whether cauliflower cheese should make it into More Home Comforts, *as it's left many people scarred for life – overcooked cauliflower with lumpy cheese sauce. When it's made properly (so easily done: blanching cauliflower, then dipping it into iced water, then reheating it in the oven), it can be a fantastic dish. The crispy maple pancetta turns it into a certain favourite in my house.*

Serves 4

1 cauliflower, cut into florets
100g unsalted butter
40g flour
500ml milk
1 tablespoon Dijon mustard
300g extra-mature Cheddar cheese, grated
sea salt and freshly ground black pepper
3 slices of brioche, blitzed to crumbs
20 rashers of pancetta or streaky bacon
2 tablespoons maple syrup

Preheat the grill to high. Bring a large pan of salted water to the boil, add the cauliflower and cook for 5–6 minutes until tender.

While the cauliflower cooks, melt 50g of the butter in a large saucepan, then whisk in the flour and cook for 1–2 minutes. Whisk in the milk slowly until you have a thick sauce, then add the mustard and half the grated cheese, and whisk until smooth. Season with salt and pepper.

Drain the cauliflower and place it in a bowl of ice-cold water to stop it cooking. Drain again and tip into an ovenproof dish. Pour the sauce over the cauliflower, top with the rest of the grated cheese, then place under the grill for 5 minutes until golden and bubbling.

While it's under the grill, heat a frying pan until hot, add the last 50g of butter, and when it's foaming, add the brioche crumbs and fry, tossing occasionally until golden-brown and crispy. Tip out into a bowl, then wipe out the pan and add all the pancetta. Fry until golden brown and crispy, then add the maple syrup and toss until sticky.

Scatter the breadcrumbs over the top of the cauliflower cheese and top with the pancetta and any remaining drizzles of maple syrup. Serve straight away.

Chicken cordon bleu

It's ham, cheese and chicken: that's all. It's a simple dish, but like many things in life, the simplest are the best. Cook the escalope in plenty of butter, not oil. By the time the butter is nut-brown, the chicken should be ready to turn over and cook on the other side. You need to allow the middle to become hot, to melt the cheese inside.

Serves 4

4 boneless skinless chicken breasts
175g Emmental cheese, cut into
  8 chunks
4 good-quality thick ham slices
75g plain flour
3 eggs, lightly beaten
150g panko breadcrumbs
sea salt and freshly ground black pepper
150g unsalted butter
300g French beans, trimmed
25g flaked almonds

Cut the chicken breasts in half widthways nearly all the way through then open out to a heart shape. Lay a large piece of clingfilm on a work surface, and place the chicken on top. Cover with another sheet of clingfilm and gently bat out with a rolling pin until about double the size and 1cm thick.

Remove the clingfilm and lay two pieces of cheese over one half of each chicken breast, then fold the ham on top. Fold the other half of the chicken over to enclose the cheese and ham, and press down lightly.

Place the flour, eggs and breadcrumbs in separate bowls, each big enough to take a chicken breast. Season the flour and eggs with salt and pepper, then pass the chicken first through the flour, then the eggs, then the breadcrumbs, coating fully.

Put 125g of the butter into a large frying pan and set over a medium heat. When the butter is just melted, add the chicken and cook for 4–5 minutes on one side until the butter is golden brown, then turn and cook for another 4–5 minutes. Baste the chicken with the melted butter as it cooks, keeping it over a medium heat. You don't want the butter or breadcrumbs to burn, and you want the chicken to be cooked all the way through and the cheese melted.

Bring a pan of salted water to the boil. Add the beans and cook for 3–4 minutes until just tender, then drain. Put the pan back on the heat and add the last of the butter and the flaked almonds. Heat until the butter is melted, then toss the beans into the butter and warm through. Season well.

Serve the chicken with the beans alongside.

Spanish beans on toast

I've never been a fan of baked beans. In my childhood I used to live on banana and chocolate flake sandwiches (don't ask!), or dripping sandwiches, while my friends tucked into baked beans when they got home from school. These days I find myself making my own beans. It's a simple recipe and one that will bring out the kid in everybody!

Serves 4–6

3 tablespoons olive oil

300g cooking chorizo sausages, roughly chopped

2 shallots, finely chopped

2 garlic cloves, finely chopped

1 red chilli, finely chopped

1 teaspoon smoked sweet paprika

1 teaspoon smoked hot paprika

400g tin chopped tomatoes

200ml chicken stock

400g tin or jar of haricot beans, drained and rinsed

400g tin or jar of large butter beans, drained and rinsed

2 tablespoons roughly chopped flat-leaf parsley

sea salt and freshly ground black pepper

4–6 thick slices of sourdough bread

2 tablespoons extra virgin olive oil

Heat a frying pan until hot, then add 2 tablespoons of the olive oil and the chopped chorizo sausages, and cook over a medium heat until just browning and the oil is turning red.

Add the shallots and cook for 2 minutes, then add the garlic, chilli and smoked paprikas, and cook for another minute before adding the tinned tomatoes. Bring to a simmer, then add the stock and beans and cook for 5–6 minutes until the sauce has thickened slightly. Add the parsley and season with salt and pepper.

Heat a griddle pan until hot, then drizzle the last tablespoon of the olive oil over the sourdough bread and toast on each side until golden.

Serve the beans and sausages spooned over the bread, with a drizzle of extra virgin olive oil.

Baked potato with bacon, taleggio and leek

Taleggio is a wonderful Italian soft cheese that looks like creamy Brie when it melts. Its flavour goes really well with potato and leek. This dish can very easily be transformed into a vegetarian one by simply omitting the bacon.

Serves 4

4 large baking potatoes, washed
1 tablespoon olive oil
sea salt and freshly ground black pepper
25g unsalted butter
1 shallot, finely diced
1 garlic clove, finely sliced
2 leeks, sliced lengthways, then across into slices
75ml white wine
300ml double cream
150g Taleggio cheese, roughly chopped
8 slices of streaky bacon

Preheat the oven to 200°C/400°F/gas mark 6.

Rub the baking potatoes with the olive oil, prick all over with a fork and place each one on a little pile of sea salt on a baking sheet. Place on the top shelf of the oven and bake for 1 hour, or until the potatoes are tender (allow more time for larger ones). Remove from the oven and leave to cool until you're able to handle them.

Meanwhile, heat a frying pan until it is medium hot. Add the butter, shallot and garlic, and cook for 2–3 minutes, then add the leeks and cook for another 2 minutes. Add the white wine and cook until reduced by half, then add the cream and cook for 3–4 minutes, until thickened. Season with salt and pepper.

When the potatoes are cool enough, cut them into quarters, place in an ovenproof dish and pour the leek sauce over the top. Slice the Taleggio and tear into pieces over the top of the sauce.

Heat a frying pan until hot. Add the bacon and cook until golden-brown, then remove, roughly chop and scatter over the top of the cheese. Place in the oven and bake for 10 minutes until golden and bubbling.

Scotch egg with homemade vegetable crisps

These are not the Scotch eggs you find in service stations all over the country – dry ones with overcooked eggs; the eggs inside these are lovely and soft-boiled. You have to be very careful and work delicately when moulding, as you don't want to break the creamy egg.

Serves 4

6 medium eggs

400g Lincolnshire sausages, skin discarded

50g plain flour, seasoned

salt and freshly ground black pepper

100g fresh breadcrumbs

1 large sweet potato, peeled and finely sliced on a mandolin

2 medium potatoes, peeled and finely sliced on a mandolin

2 raw beetroots, finely sliced on a mandolin

2 carrots, cut into fine slices with a peeler

1 jar of piccalilli, to serve

Heat a deep-fat fryer to 160°C/320°F.

Put 4 eggs into a pan of boiling water and simmer for 5 minutes until soft-boiled. Drain and place in a bowl of iced water for 10 minutes until cold. Crack the shells, then peel.

Crack the remaining 2 eggs into a bowl and beat lightly.

Divide the sausage meat into four equal portions and wrap each piece around a soft-boiled egg, pressing gently but firmly to ensure the meat covers the egg completely. Roll first in the seasoned flour, then in the beaten egg and finally in the breadcrumbs. Set aside in the fridge for 30 minutes to chill, then reshape slightly to ensure the meat clings tightly around the egg.

Drop them into the fat fryer and cook for 7–8 minutes until golden and the meat is cooked through. Drain on kitchen paper and set aside while you cook the crisps.

Drop the sliced vegetables into the fryer in batches and cook for 2–3 minutes until cooked through and golden. Drain on kitchen paper and season with salt and pepper.

Cut the Scotch eggs in half and serve with piccalilli and the vegetable crisps.

Cottage pie

If you asked me for one dish aside from steak and chips that I'd be happy cooking for any big-name chef who ventures into my kitchen at home, this would be it. The key is in its simplicity: good-quality slow-cooked beef, fantastic mashed potato, cooked with care and attention, and fresh peas. Life just does not get any better. All chefs love the crispy edges, so don't clean the dish before serving! Those are the best bits.

Serves 4

8 medium baking potatoes

1 tablespoon vegetable oil, plus extra for rubbing

rock salt

600g minced beef

2 onions, finely chopped

3 garlic cloves, finely chopped

4 sprigs of thyme, leaves picked and finely chopped

1 celery stick, finely diced

2 tablespoons tomato purée

Worcestershire sauce, to taste

9 carrots, unpeeled

100ml red wine

500ml beef stock

salt and freshly ground black pepper

50g caster sugar

125g unsalted butter

150ml milk

Preheat the oven to 190°C/375°F/gas mark 5.

Prick the potatoes all over with a fork, then rub with a little oil. Set them on a bed of rock salt in a tray and bake for 1–1½ hours, or until tender.

Heat a large sauté pan until hot. Add the vegetable oil and fry the beef until just browned. Add the onions, garlic, thyme and celery, and fry for a couple of minutes until softened. Add the tomato purée and cook for 1–2 minutes, then add the Worcestershire sauce and one of the carrots, finely diced. Add the red wine and cook until reduced by one-third, then add the beef stock and bring to a simmer, stirring occasionally. Cook for 30 minutes until the beef is tender and the sauce has thickened. Tip the mince into a bowl and season to taste with salt and pepper, and as much Worcestershire sauce as you like. Set aside in the fridge to cool while you make the mash.

While the beef cools, top and tail the remaining carrots and place them in a pan half filled with water. Add a pinch of salt, the sugar and a knob of butter, bring to the boil, then reduce to a gentle simmer and cook for 30–40 minutes until soft. The liquid should evaporate, leaving a lovely glaze to the carrots.

When the potatoes are cooked and just cool enough to handle, slice them in half, scoop out the flesh and pass through a potato ricer into a bowl. Turn the oven up to 220°C/425°F/gas mark 7. Add almost all the remaining butter to the potatoes and warm the milk in a saucepan until just simmering. Pour onto the potatoes and beat until the mash is smooth and creamy. Season to taste with salt and pepper.

Pour the cooled mince into a baking dish and spoon the hot mash over the top, fluffing the top with a fork. Scatter over a few dots of butter, then place in the oven for 10–15 minutes, until golden-brown and piping hot throughout.

Serve with the carrots.

Ham, fried egg, beer mustard and homemade chips

Making your own mustard is easy and once you see just how easy it is, I reckon a few of you might take it up as a business. Mixing and matching the flavours is great fun too. I often make it at home to give away as a gift.

Serves 4

vegetable oil, for deep-frying

400g chipping potatoes, peeled and cut into batons 1 x 1cm and 6cm long

1 tablespoon vegetable oil

4 eggs

½ cooked ham hock, shredded (see page 51), or thickly sliced good-quality cooked ham

sea salt

For the mustard

75g clear honey

50g soft light brown sugar

100ml good-quality white wine vinegar

75g black mustard seeds

75g yellow mustard seeds

100ml beer

To make the mustard, place the honey, sugar and vinegar in a saucepan and heat until the honey has dissolved.

Put the mustard seeds and beer into a bowl and pour over the warm honey mixture, then stir to combine and set aside in the fridge for 2 hours, or even overnight.

Pour into a food processor and blitz to a purée – it takes a good 5 minutes, then the seeds will break down and the mustard will become creamy.

Spoon into a sterilised jar, seal and keep in the fridge for up to two weeks.

Heat a deep-fat fryer to 160°C/320°F. Place the potatoes in the fryer and cook for 8–10 minutes until light golden-brown and cooked through.

Meanwhile, heat a frying pan until hot and add the vegetable oil. Crack the eggs directly into the pan, then leave to fry, spooning the oil over the top of the eggs occasionally until just set and crisping around the edges. Add the ham to the pan as the eggs fry, to heat through and crisp slightly.

Drain the chips on kitchen paper and sprinkle with sea salt.

Pile the chips onto plates, place an egg alongside, shred some ham hock next to it and finish with a dollop of mustard.

Fresh crab and chilli linguine

People often ask me what my own personal food heaven or food hell would be. One of my top three for food heaven would definitely be fresh crab. There's nothing better than fresh white crabmeat served with just a touch of lemon. This linguine dish takes it one step further, with a spicy hit from the chilli: simple yet full of flavour. You could use dark crabmeat or a combination of the two; just make sure it's very good quality.

Serves 4

300g dried linguine
50ml olive oil
2 shallots, finely chopped
2 garlic cloves, finely chopped
1 red chilli, finely chopped
½ teaspoon crushed red chilli flakes
100g fresh brown crabmeat, picked
300g fresh white crabmeat, picked
100ml white wine
2 tablespoons roughly chopped
    flat-leaf parsley
1 lemon, zested and juiced
sea salt and freshly ground black pepper
1–2 tablespoons extra virgin olive oil

Cook the linguine according to the packet instructions, then drain, reserving 100ml of the pasta water.

Heat a large sauté pan until hot. Add the olive oil, shallots, garlic, chilli and chilli flakes, and sweat for 3–4 minutes until softened. Add the crabmeat and toss to combine, then add the white wine and cook until the wine has reduced by half and the crab is hot through. Add the parsley and lemon zest, and toss together, then add lemon juice, salt and black pepper to taste.

Add the drained pasta and the reserved pasta water, and toss together, checking the seasoning once more.

Divide between serving plates and serve with a drizzle of extra virgin olive oil.

I've been privileged in my time to work with some of the best and most influential chefs and cooks that Britain has ever produced. One of these was the late, great Marguerite Patten, not only a wonderful person but a highly knowledgeable cook with thousands of books and leaflets sold. She was one of the people who gave people something to look forward to at the dinner table after the Second World War. Marguerite was an inspiration to so many and will be sadly missed. This simple fish pie is a tribute to her.

Fish pie with peas

Serves 6–8

8 baking potatoes
1 tablespoon vegetable oil
rock salt
1 onion, thinly sliced
½ teaspoon black peppercorns
2 bay leaves
500g smoked haddock, boneless and skinless
400g haddock, boneless and skinless
400g cod, boneless and skinless
200g unsalted butter
3 heaped tablespoons plain flour
475ml milk
1 lemon, zested and juiced
sea salt and freshly ground black pepper
1 small bunch of flat-leaf parsley, roughly chopped
250g frozen cooked peeled prawns, defrosted and drained
200g frozen peas

Preheat the oven to 180°C/350°F/gas mark 4.

Prick the potatoes all over with a fork, then rub with a little oil and set on a bed of rock salt in a tray and bake for 1–1½ hours, or until tender.

Half fill a deep sauté pan with 1 litre of water and set over a high heat, then add the onion, black peppercorns and bay leaves. When it's simmering, add the smoked haddock, haddock and cod, return to the boil, then gently simmer for 3–4 minutes.

Lift the fish out with a slotted spoon into a colander set over a large bowl, then place the colander on a plate to catch any other juices. Place a fine sieve over the bowl and strain the cooking liquor into it, discarding the onion, peppercorns and bay leaves.

Clean the pan out and return to the heat. Add 100g of the butter and when it's melted, add the flour and cook for 1 minute until light golden-brown. Add 50ml of the milk and mix to a paste, then add another 350ml of the milk and cook until thickened.

Add 750ml of the reserved stock to the pan and cook for 5 minutes until the sauce is smooth and just thick enough to coat the back of a spoon. Discard the rest of the stock, or chill it and use in another dish. Add the lemon zest and juice, season to taste with salt and pepper, then remove from the heat.

Flake the fish into the sauce, keeping it in reasonably large pieces, then add the parsley and lightly mix together. Add the prawns and stir through, then spoon into a large ovenproof dish. Turn the oven up to 220°C/425°F/gas mark 7.

When the potatoes are cooked and just cool enough to handle, cut them in half, scoop out the flesh and pass through a potato ricer into a sauté pan. Warm up with 75g of the butter and the last 75ml of milk – it needs to be a smooth thick mash, not too soft – beating until smooth. Spoon the mash into a piping bag fitted with a large star nozzle and pipe over the top of the fish.

Place on a baking sheet in the oven and bake for 5–10 minutes until golden and hot through. (Or, if preparing in advance and chilling, bake for 30 minutes until piping hot.)

While the pie heats through, bring a pan of salted water to the boil, add the peas and cook for 2–3 minutes until tender. Drain and return to the pan, add the remaining butter and season to taste.

Serve the pie with the peas.

I've said throughout this book that I've learnt so much from so many chefs throughout my travels, and a classic Italian ragu is one example. The essence of all Italian cooking is top-quality ingredients; gently cooking over a period of time creates this wonderful dish. Finish cooking the linguine in the ragu itself; this is definitely not dry 'spag bol' with a dollop of sauce over the top. By mixing it in, each spoonful tastes as good as the last. I love my pasta machine, but you can roll the pasta by hand – or cheat and buy fresh pasta.

Linguine with beef ragu

Serves 4

For James's pasta

1kg '00' flour
1kg semolina flour
12 eggs

For pasta made the usual way

300g '00' flour, plus extra for dusting
3 eggs

For the ragu

2 tablespoons olive oil
1 onion, finely chopped
2 garlic cloves, finely chopped
1 large carrot, finely chopped
1 celery stick, finely chopped
200g smoked bacon lardons
500g minced beef
2 tablespoons tomato purée
400g tin chopped tomatoes
150ml red wine
a handful of basil leaves, roughly torn
sea salt and freshly ground black
   pepper
3–4 tablespoons freshly grated
   Parmesan cheese

To make pasta my way, tip the flours and eggs into a large pasta machine, turn on and leave until the mixture has a breadcrumb-like texture. Turn the extruder on and let the pasta push out to form linguine.

To make pasta the usual way, place the flour on a work surface, make a well in the centre, then crack the eggs into the well and gradually draw in the flour to form a sticky dough. Keep working it until all the flour is incorporated and the dough is smooth.

Alternatively, place the flour and eggs in a food processor and pulse until the mixture forms small crumbs. Tip out onto a work surface and squish into a ball, then knead for a few minutes until smooth. Wrap in clingfilm and chill for 20 minutes in the fridge.

Lightly flour the business end of a pasta machine. Cut the pasta into three equal pieces and flatten out to about 1cm thick. Starting at the lowest (thickest) setting, feed the dough through the machine, turning the handle with one hand and holding the dough as it comes through the machine with the other.

Change the setting on the pasta machine to the next-thinnest setting, flour it again and feed the pasta sheet through the machine again, as before.

Repeat this process three or four more times, flouring the machine and changing

the setting down each time until the last-but-one setting. Fold the pasta over into a manageable size, then cut through it lengthways to form strips about 3mm thick. Hang over a clean broom handle or the back of a chair so that the pasta can dry slightly while you make the ragu.

Heat a large sauté pan or casserole dish until hot. Add the olive oil, onion and garlic, and sweat for a couple of minutes. Add the carrot and celery, and cook for another couple of minutes, then add the bacon and fry for 1 minute. Add the beef mince and fry until just browned through.

Add the tomato purée, cook for 1 minute, then add the tinned tomatoes and red wine and bring to a simmer. Add half the basil, stir well and cook for 45 minutes until tender and thickened. Season with salt and pepper, then stir in the last of the basil.

Bring a large pan of salted water to the boil. Add the pasta and cook for 3–4 minutes until tender. Drain and add to the pan of ragu, toss well and serve with Parmesan sprinkled over the top.

Hot tinned Serrano, mozzarella and rocket pesto sandwich

I don't know where this idea came from – maybe it was watching Bear Grylls on TV as he was climbing a mountain with his food in a tin box! This is a simple sandwich that can be reheated using a disposable barbecue. If you don't want to make your own bread, just use a good bought loaf.

Serves 4–6

For the bread sponge

50g very strong flour
50g durum wheat semolina flour
6g fresh yeast
¼ teaspoon caster sugar
90ml tepid water

For the bread

unsalted butter, for greasing
450g very strong flour
450g durum wheat semolina flour
2½ teaspoons sea salt
475ml tepid water

For the hot tinned sandwich

150g rocket leaves
a large bunch of basil
1 garlic clove, peeled
50g parmesan cheese, grated
125ml extra virgin olive oil
50g pine nuts, toasted
freshly ground black pepper
3 balls of mozzarella cheese, drained and
   thinly sliced
150g sliced Serrano ham

To make the bread sponge, put the flour, semolina flour, yeast and sugar into a bowl and mix well. Add the water and whisk to form a thick batter. Cover and set aside to ferment for 1½ hours.

To make the bread, put the fermented sponge into a kitchen mixer fitted with a dough hook, add the flour, semolina flour and salt, then start the machine running. Add about two-thirds of the water to start the dough, then add the remainder of the water a little at a time until a soft dough forms. Tip the dough onto a floured work surface and knead for a few minutes until smooth, then put back into the bowl and leave to prove for 1½ hours.

Knock the air out of the dough and divide in half, then knead lightly and form into a long sausage with pointed ends. Transfer to a baking sheet and cut slashes along the top. Repeat with the other half of the dough, then set aside to prove for 1 hour.

Preheat the oven to 220°C/425°F/gas mark 7. Bake the bread for 45 minutes, then set aside to cool before slicing.

To make your hot tinned sandwich, preheat the oven to 200°C/400°F/gas mark 6, or light a barbecue and leave until the coals are glowing. Line a 1kg loaf tin with buttered silver foil.

Place three-quarters of the rocket, half the basil, the garlic, Parmesan and olive oil in a food processor or a pestle and mortar and blitz to a fine purée. Add the pine nuts and black pepper to taste, and blitz again until well combined.

Lay two slices of bread out on a work surface and spread with some of the pesto. Layer on the rest of the rocket and basil, the mozzarella and Serrano ham, then top with another slice of bread. Spread with pesto, then repeat, layering up with the remaining ingredients until you have two piles.

Place the two piles of sandwiches along the length of the lined loaf tin, squeezing them together slightly so that they fit snugly. Fold the foil over the top so that everything is enclosed, then place in the oven or on the barbecue for 30 minutes, until hot through.

To serve, simply unwrap the tin and pull the sandwiches out.

Corned beef hash with beer-battered onion rings

I don't understand why so many chefs sneer at tinned produce – corned beef is a stalwart of my larder. With crispy onion rings on top, corned beef is always a favourite in my house.

Serves 6

vegetable oil, for deep-frying

4 medium potatoes, peeled and diced into cubes

100g plain flour

1 tablespoon caster sugar

sea salt and freshly ground black pepper

2 tablespoons cider vinegar

150–200ml beer

50g unsalted butter

2 onions

1 garlic clove, crushed

4 tomatoes

340g tinned corned beef, roughly chopped

1 tablespoon Worcestershire sauce

4–5 drops of Tabasco sauce

Heat a deep-fat fryer to 190°C/375°F, or heat the oil for deep-frying in a deep heavy-based saucepan until a breadcrumb sizzles and turns brown when dropped into it. (CAUTION: hot oil can be dangerous. Do not leave unattended.)

Put the potatoes into a saucepan and cover with water. Bring to the boil, then simmer for 8–10 minutes until just tender. Drain and set aside.

While the potatoes are cooking, make the onion rings. Put the flour, sugar, a pinch of salt, the vinegar and 100ml of the beer into a bowl and whisk to a thick batter, then gradually add more beer until the batter is the consistency of double cream. Cut one onion into 1cm thick rings and drop into the batter, tossing to coat, then carefully place in batches in the hot oil and cook for 3–4 minutes. Drain on kitchen paper.

Chop the remaining onion, then heat a frying pan until medium hot. Add half the butter and the chopped onion and cook for 2–3 minutes until softened. Add the garlic, the drained potatoes and the rest of the butter and fry for 2–3 minutes.

Chop two of the tomatoes, then add them to the pan with the corned beef and stir-fry until softened and hot through. Add the Worcestershire sauce and Tabasco and season to taste with salt and pepper.

Slice the last two tomatoes and lay on serving plates, then spoon the hash alongside and finish with a pile of onion rings on top.

One of the first things I did when I moved into the house was dig the foundations for the greenhouse. Both my granddad and uncle had greenhouses at the bottom of the garden and taught me so much about growing amazing produce. Over the years we've just about mastered the art of growing tomatoes, often ending up with SO many of them! This is a great dish for using up a glut of seasonal tomatoes. Just purée them, then hang the purée in muslin or a tea towel and let it drip down into a bowl below. The flavour is incredible. You can also freeze it and use it for Bloody Marys.

Tomato consommé

Serves 4–6

2kg ripe tomatoes, chopped
2 shallots, roughly chopped
½ teaspoon Tabasco sauce
1 tablespoon Worcestershire sauce
a small handful of basil leaves
sea salt
12 mixed heritage tomatoes, halved or quartered
1 tablespoon tiny basil leaves

Place the chopped tomatoes, shallots, Tabasco, Worcestershire sauce and basil leaves in a food processor and blitz for 8–10 seconds, until just broken up but not puréed – a bit like gazpacho. Season with salt, then pulse again and check the seasoning once more.

Line a colander with a large piece of muslin, then set it over a large bowl. Tip the tomato mixture into the muslin and seal with pegs or string, then place in the fridge and leave to drip through for at least 4 hours or overnight, without pressing or squeezing at all.

Lift out the muslin bag (don't discard the contents, you can make a great tomato sauce with it – just add a little olive oil and cook for 15 minutes). Check the tomato consommé for flavour balance, adding extra Tabasco and Worcestershire sauce as desired. Cover and chill in the fridge until ready to serve.

Ladle into bowls, and garnish with the pieces of heritage tomato and a scattering of tiny basil leaves.

Tip: You can serve this cold or warm, and if you have any left over, freeze it in ice cube trays to use in a Bloody Mary.

French onion soup with cheesy croutons

Whenever I go to France I make a beeline for Le Fouquet's on the Champs-Elysées, in the shadow of the Arc de Triomphe. The keys to a good onion soup like this are the stock and the cooking time, plus a little sherry. Get those three things right and it's the best-tasting soup out there, plus of course the melted cheese croutons on the top.

Serves 4

3 tablespoons olive oil
3 large onions, finely sliced
2 sprigs of thyme, leaves picked
1 tablespoon soft brown sugar
2 garlic cloves, finely sliced
200ml white wine
1 heaped tablespoon plain flour
50ml brandy
50ml dry sherry
1 litre fresh dark beef stock
½ baguette, sliced thickly into chunks
sea salt and freshly ground black pepper
110g Gruyère cheese, grated

Heat a large sauté pan until hot, then add 2 tablespoons of the olive oil, the onions, thyme and soft brown sugar, and fry for 10–15 minutes over a medium–low heat, or until the onions are softened and golden-brown, stirring occasionally so they don't catch on the bottom of the pan.

Add the garlic and cook for 1 minute, then add the white wine and cook until reduced by half. Stir in the flour and cook for 2 minutes. Add the brandy and sherry, then pour in the stock and bring to the boil. Reduce the heat slightly and cook gently for about 10–15 minutes.

While the soup simmers, heat a griddle until hot. Drizzle the remaining oil over the bread and toast on one side, then set aside.

Check the seasoning of the soup, adding plenty of salt and a little pepper, and adding more sugar or alcohol if necessary to suit your own taste.

Preheat the grill to high. Ladle the soup into bowls and top with the toasted bread, then add the cheese and return to the grill until bubbling and golden-brown.

Any leftover soup can be frozen for up to four weeks.

Mrs Baxter's chicken livers

This was the dish that got me into so much trouble at school. Little did my twelve-year-old self know that bringing in a bottle of alcohol was going to be such a problem! It tasted nice though – the dish I mean.

Serves 2–3

1 slice of white bread
1 tablespoon olive oil
7 slices of dry-cured streaky bacon
400g chicken livers, trimmed
50ml brandy
1 tablespoon sherry vinegar
50ml double cream
50g mangetout, sliced
sea salt and freshly ground black pepper
2 handfuls of rocket leaves

Heat a griddle pan until hot. Drizzle both sides of the bread with the olive oil, then place on the griddle, toast on both sides and set aside.

Heat a frying pan until warm, then add the bacon and cook until golden brown and crisp. Lift out onto a plate and set aside. Dip the bread in the hot bacon fat in the pan, then set aside again.

Return the frying pan to the heat, then add the chicken livers and cook for 2–3 minutes until browned on the outside but still pink on the inside. Deglaze the pan with the brandy, then add the sherry vinegar, cream and mangetout, and cook for a couple of minutes. Season with salt and pepper.

Pile the rocket into a serving bowl, then roughly chop the toasted bread and the crispy bacon, and scatter over the top. Spoon the chicken livers and juices over and serve straight away.

Cheddar, smoked bacon and courgette quiches

There are a couple of quiches in this book: when they're made with good-quality ingredients, including courgettes freshly picked from the garden, there's little better for a lunchtime snack. The key is in the cooking: nice, thin pastry (you don't need to bake it blind, just reduce the temperature and bake it for longer).

Serves 6

For the pastry

250g plain flour, plus extra for dusting
150g cold unsalted butter, cubed
a pinch of sea salt
1 egg, beaten

For the filling

6 slices of dry-cured smoked streaky bacon
5 egg yolks
300ml double cream
sea salt and freshly ground black pepper
75g mature Cheddar cheese, finely grated
1 small courgette, finely diced
4 sprigs of thyme, leaves picked

For the salad

1 teaspoon grainy mustard
1 teaspoon red wine vinegar
3 teaspoons rapeseed oil
1 bag of salad leaves
1 head of little gem lettuce, leaves picked

To make the pastry, put the flour into a bowl, add the butter and rub together with your fingertips until breadcrumbs form. Add the salt and egg, and bring together, then knead very lightly to form a soft dough. Cover and place in the fridge for 10–15 minutes to firm up.

Preheat the oven to 180°C/350°F/gas mark 4 and grease six loose-bottomed tart tins 9cm in diameter and 4cm deep.

Roll the pastry out on a lightly floured surface to a thickness of 3mm and cut it into six discs larger than the tart tins, re-rolling the last of the pastry for the last two tins. Lay the pastry over the tins and press gently into the base and sides. Trim the sides so the pastry is flush to the edge.

For the filling, heat a frying pan until medium–hot, then add the bacon and fry for 3–4 minutes, until golden-brown and just crispy. Drain on kitchen paper, then roughly chop and set aside.

Whisk the egg yolks and cream together, whisk once more, then season with salt and pepper. Sprinkle half the cheese into the bottom of the tart cases, and follow with half the bacon, the courgette, then the last of the cheese and bacon. Finish with a little thyme, then pull the oven rack out slightly and set the tins near the edge. Pour in the egg mixture, then slide the quiches fully into the oven and bake for 15–20 minutes until just set and golden-brown. Remove and cool slightly before serving.

For the salad, put the mustard, vinegar and rapeseed oil into a small jar with a lid, and shake vigorously to emulsify together. Put the salad into a resealable bag, then, when ready to serve, tip the dressing into the bag and shake to coat all the leaves.

Serve the quiches at room temperature, with the salad.

Posh Comforts

Pork and hazelnut terrine with apricot and tomato chutney

People are so often put off making terrines and pâtés until they realise how easy they are, and this one is even simpler than most, as it uses good-quality sausage meat as its base. You can make it with venison sausages and add whatever flavouring you like.

Serves 6

For the pastry

275g plain flour, plus extra for dusting
50g strong white flour
1¼ teaspoons salt
65g unsalted butter
75g lard
1 egg, lightly beaten

For the filling

1kg pork and apple sausages, skins removed
1 banana shallot, finely chopped
2 tablespoons roughly chopped flat-leaf parsley
100g toasted hazelnuts, roughly chopped

For the chutney

150g light muscovado sugar
1 onion, finely chopped
3 tomatoes, roughly chopped
200g soft dried apricots, roughly chopped
½ teaspoon dried chilli flakes
125ml white wine vinegar
sea salt and freshly ground black pepper

To serve

1 bunch of radishes

Preheat the oven to 200°C/400°F/gas mark 6. Grease a 23 x 10cm terrine mould.

Start by making the pastry. Put both flours and the salt into a bowl.

Pour 175ml of water into a small saucepan, add the butter and lard, and bring to the boil over a low heat until the fats have melted. Pour the mixture onto the flour and stir together until it forms a soft dough. Tip onto a lightly floured board and knead very gently until smooth and cooled slightly. Cut one-third of the dough off and set aside while you make the pie.

Roll the remaining pastry out so that it's as big as the terrine, then gently lay it inside, pressing it into each corner and pulling the pastry so that it comes all the way up the sides of the terrine. Place in the fridge while you make the filling.

Put the sausage meat into a large bowl, then add the shallot, parsley and hazelnuts, and mix well to combine. Spoon a little at a time into the pastry-lined terrine, pressing gently into the corners to make sure there are no gaps.

Take the remaining pastry and roll it out so that it's big enough to fit the top of the terrine. Brush the edges of the pastry in the terrine mould with the beaten egg, then lay the pastry rectangle on top and crimp together at the edges. Decorate with any remaining pastry. Brush with the remaining egg wash and pierce a hole in the centre of the pie, then bake for 1–1¼ hours.

To make the chutney, heat a large frying pan until hot, add the sugar and cook until totally dissolved and starting to caramelise.

Stir in the onion, tomatoes, apricots and dried chilli flakes, then deglaze with the vinegar – the mixture will become lumpy, but continue cooking until the lumps dissolve. Boil gently for 5–10 minutes, until the fruit and veg are tender and the mixture has thickened slightly. Season with salt and pepper. You can use it straight away, or decant it into a sterilised jar and keep it in the fridge for two weeks.

When the terrine is cooked, remove it from the mould and either serve immediately, or chill and serve cold. Slice and serve with a dollop of chutney and a few radishes.

I don't really like the phrase 'signature dish', but if we had one in the restaurant this would be it. It's a favourite both of the chefs who cook it and the guests who eat it. Pearl barley replaces the rice in this, and we make a purée of parsley or, when in season, wild garlic, which we fold through the 'risotto' to give it a beautiful rich colour and distinct flavour.

Pearl barley risotto with beer-braised beef cheeks and onion

Serves 4

For the braised cheeks

2 beef cheeks, fully trimmed
2 garlic cloves, crushed
1 bay leaf
1 small bunch of thyme
500ml strong full-flavoured ale
2 tablespoons vegetable oil
2 litres beef stock
sea salt and freshly ground black pepper
1 beef stock cube

For the garnish

2 small white onions, peeled and halved
500ml strong full-flavoured ale
4 sticks of salsify, washed
1 lemon, halved
50g butter

For the risotto

2 garlic cloves, lightly crushed
200g pearl barley, soaked in cold water
    for 1 hour, then drained
1 litre hot chicken stock
100g flat-leaf parsley, roughly chopped
100ml double cream
25g Parmesan cheese, finely grated
sea salt and freshly ground black pepper

Put the beef cheeks into a large bowl, add the garlic, bay leaf and thyme, and pour the beer over the top. Cover and place in the fridge to marinate for at least 6 hours, if not overnight.

Preheat the oven to 150°C/300°F/gas mark 2.

Lift the cheeks out of the marinade and cut them in half. Heat an ovenproof casserole dish until hot, add the vegetable oil and the cheeks, and fry on each side until dark, brown. Pour in the reserved marinade and the beef stock, and bring to a simmer. Cover with foil, then place in the oven and braise gently for 6 hours until the cheeks are very tender and the liquid has reduced and thickened – this is a great one for the slow cooker, set on low for 12 hours or overnight.

Lift the cheeks out of the sauce and set aside, then return the casserole dish to a medium heat and bring the sauce to the boil. Cook until the sauce has thickened enough to coat the back of a spoon, then season well with salt and pepper. Return the beef cheeks to the thickened sauce and keep warm until ready to serve.

To make the garnish, put the onions and beer into a small saucepan, bring to the boil, then simmer gently for 45 minutes until the onions are tender all the way through. Leave to cool in the beer while you prepare the salsify.

Peel the salsify and cut into batons 5cm long, one at a time, then drop straight away into a bowl of cold water with the lemon halves in it. Put a pan of water on to boil, add the salsify and a squeeze of lemon juice from the bowl and simmer for 8–10 minutes until just tender – you can check with the tip of a knife. Drain and set aside until ready to serve.

To make the risotto, put the garlic and barley, and enough hot chicken stock to just cover the barley, into a saucepan and bring to a simmer. Cook for 10–12 minutes until the barley is tender.

While the barley cooks, put the parsley and 125ml of chicken stock into a blender and blitz to a very fine purée – this will take a good while. Add the parsley purée to the cooked barley, then add the cream and Parmesan, and heat through. Check the seasoning, then remove from the heat – you want to keep it green.

Heat a frying pan until hot and add the butter. When it's foaming, add the halved onions and fry until just golden brown, then add the salsify and fry until browned.

Spoon some of the barley risotto into the centre of each plate. Place a beef cheek in the middle of the risotto, then separate out the petals of the onions and scatter a few around. Add the salsify around the edge, then crumble a tiny bit of beef stock cube on top of the beef cheek.

Lemongrass poussin with red cabbage salad

This is one of my all-time favourite meals, and it was great cooking it with my great friend Pierre Koffmann on the show – thanks to all his help, the dressing is off the scale!

Serves 4

2 lemongrass stems, finely chopped

2 tablespoons roughly chopped coriander leaves

4 garlic cloves, finely chopped

2 red chillies, finely chopped

5cm piece of ginger, peeled and grated

2 limes, juiced

300ml vegetable oil

4 poussins

1 egg yolk

2 teaspoons Dijon mustard

2 teaspoons red wine vinegar or walnut vinegar

sea salt and freshly ground black pepper

1 small red cabbage, very finely sliced

Soak a clean wooden broomstick in cold water, overnight preferably. Set a barbecue going and wait until the flames have died down.

Place the lemongrass, coriander, garlic, chillies, ginger and lime juice in a bowl with 50ml of the vegetable oil, and mix to combine. Toss the poussins in this marinade, scooping some inside too. Slide them onto the centre of the soaked broomstick and tie each one with string to secure them onto the stick.

Set the broomstick over the barbecue, about 30cm above the coals, and cook for 30 minutes, turning every so often to cook each side all the way through. If you want to cook the poussins in the oven, put them in a roasting tray and roast for 30–40 minutes at 200°C/400°F/gas mark 6.

While the poussins cook, make the salad. Whisk the egg yolk, Dijon mustard, vinegar and 250ml of water together in a bowl until combined. Add the rest of the oil gradually, whisking all the time until emulsified. Season well with salt and pepper.

Place the red cabbage in a bowl, add 100ml of the dressing and toss to combine. Check the seasoning, then set aside until ready to serve. This salad can be made up to a day in advance. The remainder of the dressing can be kept in a sealed container in the fridge for up to one week.

To check that the poussins are cooked through, insert the point of a knife or the prongs of a carving fork into the thigh and check that they're hot all the way through. If not, keep roasting for another 5 minutes and check again.

Serve with a pile of red cabbage salad.

Home-smoked trout with feta salad

I'm lucky enough to live near the home of river trout, the River Test in Hampshire, and I've fished on the river a few times in search of the prize – the great brown trout. When I do catch one – and it doesn't happen often – this is one of the dishes I make. Smoked trout has a milder flavour and to me is less strong than salmon. Home-smoking is actually very easy and gives a wonderful flavour that you can't get in the bought stuff.

Serves 4–6

100g caster sugar

200g sea salt

1 large trout, cleaned, filleted and pin-boned

1 tablespoon white balsamic vinegar

3 tablespoons extra virgin olive oil

sea salt and freshly ground black pepper

2 shallots, cut into rings

200g cooked beetroots, roughly chopped

200g feta cheese, roughly chopped

100g watercress

Mix the sugar and sea salt together in a bowl. Place a couple of pieces of clingfilm on top of each other on a work surface, then sprinkle a quarter of the salt sugar mixture onto the centre in a line. Place one trout fillet, skin-side down, on the salt sugar and cover with one-third of the remaining mixture, then cover with the clingfilm. Repeat with the other fillet and the rest of the salt sugar. Place on a tray in the fridge for 12–24 hours.

Remove the trout from the clingfilm and brush off the salt sugar mixture. Rinse the fish thoroughly under cold running water, then pat dry.

Place three lit candles underneath a bucket barbecue with holes at the bottom. Cover the base with foil, then sprinkle over a generous handful of oak chips. Drizzle with a little water, then place a grate over the top and lay the trout, skin-side down, in the centre. Cover with a lid and leave to smoke for 1½ hours, checking that the chips are smouldering, not burning. Remove and allow to cool.

Whisk the vinegar and olive oil together, and season with salt and pepper.

Place the shallot rings, beetroots and feta on a plate, and flake the smoked trout over the top. Finish with the watercress leaves and a drizzle of dressing.

Carpaccio of tuna with caramelised watermelon

This is one of my favourite fish dishes – it's so simple. The idea comes from a dish I had in a restaurant in New York when I was there on a bit of a food tour. It's a simpler dish made this way, but the taste is great and it can be made at home. The keys to it are fresh tuna and really good extra virgin olive oil.

Serves 4

¼ watermelon, peeled and cut into 1cm thick slices
sea salt and freshly ground black pepper
2 thin slices of sourdough bread
4 x 50–75g fresh tuna loin steaks
1 lemon, juiced
2 tablespoons very finely chopped chives
1 shallot, very finely chopped
50g unsalted butter
2 tablespoons extra virgin olive oil

Place the watermelon in a resealable bag with a pinch of salt and place in the fridge for two to three days.

Preheat the oven to 150°C/300°F/gas mark 2.

Toast the bread in a toaster, then slice in half horizontally so you have one toasted side and one untoasted side. Place between two thin baking trays and bake in the oven for 5 minutes until crisp. Remove and cool between the trays.

Spread a sheet of clingfilm on a work surface and lay a piece of tuna on it, then cover with a second sheet of clingfilm. Bat the tuna very gently with a rolling pin so that you have an evenly thin piece, finishing by rolling it flat – about 2mm thick. Repeat with each piece of tuna.

Take a bowl the same size as the centre of the plate you are going to serve on, then turn it upside down and place it on one of the pieces of clingfilmed tuna. Cut around the bowl so you are left with a disc of tuna, then set the disc aside. Repeat with the rest of the tuna. Remove the clingfilm from the trimmings, then chop them very finely and place in a bowl.

Add a squeeze of lemon juice, two-thirds of the chives and shallot, season with salt and pepper, and mix together to form a tuna tartare.

Slice the watermelon into pieces. Heat a frying pan until hot, add the butter, and only when it's nut-brown add the watermelon and fry on each side for 1 minute, or until browned and hot through. Add a pinch of salt and tip onto a plate.

Place a spoonful of tuna tartare on each piece of toast and place a piece of the fried watermelon on top. Place on a serving plate. Lift the clingfilm off one side of the tuna discs and flip over. Lay them on top of the tartare and lift off the second sheet of clingfilm. Drizzle with the extra virgin olive oil and brush it all over the tuna.

Garnish with the rest of the shallot and chives, and add a squeeze of lemon juice and some pepper.

Ricotta and herb cappellacci with pesto, peas and beans

Serves 4

For the cappellacci

400g '00' pasta flour

4 eggs, plus 1–2 tablespoons water if needed

200g ricotta cheese, drained

1 tablespoon freshly grated Parmesan cheese, plus to serve

4 teaspoons finely chopped chives

1 tablespoon finely chopped basil leaves

1 teaspoon finely chopped marjoram leaves

1 teaspoon finely chopped oregano leaves

sea salt and freshly ground black pepper

For the pesto, peas and beans

60g basil leaves

1 garlic clove, finely chopped

50g Parmesan cheese, grated

75ml extra virgin olive oil

100g fresh peas

100g runner beans, cut into 2cm pieces

a few sprigs of mint

To make the cappellacci, place the flour and eggs in a bowl or food processor and rub together or pulse until the mixture forms small crumbs. Remove from the processor, if using, pull together to form a dough, then knead lightly for 2–3 minutes, until the dough is smooth and elastic. Cover and place in the fridge for 20 minutes – you can cut the pasta you don't wish to use into portions and freeze any extra.

Meanwhile, place the ricotta, Parmesan and herbs in a bowl, and mix to combine then season to taste with salt and pepper.

Roll out the pasta to 2mm thick, using a pasta machine or by hand with a rolling pin. Lay a sheet of pasta on the work surface and cut into 7.5cm squares. Brush one of the squares lightly with a little water around the edges, then place a spoonful of the ricotta mixture in the centre. Fold the pasta over the filling to form a triangle and press lightly around the edges to seal. Pressing gently on the edges, carefully roll the back long edge of the triangle up and over the filled area. Twist the two long ends of the triangle around, away from the tip, then press the long ends together, using a little more water to seal if necessary. Repeat with the remaining pasta and filling.

To make the pesto, place the basil, garlic and parmesan in a food processor or a pestle and mortar and blitz to a fine purée. Add the olive oil and blitz again until well combined. Check the seasoning, then tip into a sauté pan. Bring a pan of salted water to the boil, add the peas and beans, and simmer for 3–4 minutes until tender. Drain and tip into the sauté pan with the pesto.

Bring a large pan of salted water to the boil, add the cappellacci and cook for 1–2 minutes until they float to the top of the pan. Lift out with a slotted spoon and add them to the pesto, peas and beans, then add a couple of spoonfuls of pasta water and toss well to combine and warm the whole dish through.

Serve with extra Parmesan grated over the top and a few sprigs of mint.

Grilled mackerel with dulse butter and summer veg stew

Seaweed is one of the joys of cooking, and it can be a great way to season and reduce the amount of salt you add to your diet. And dulse is amazing – added to food like this the taste is simple and clean. I've been to harvest the stuff off the south Welsh coast, but it's found all over the British Isles and you can buy it, mainly dried.

Serves 2

20g dulse seaweed
175g unsalted butter, softened
½ lemon, juiced
2 mackerel, gutted
1 shallot, finely sliced
75g podded broad beans
100g fresh peas, half podded, half opened but left in the pod
12 asparagus spears, trimmed
4 sprigs of tarragon, leaves picked
freshly ground black pepper

Preheat the grill to high.

Soak the dulse in cold water for about 10 seconds, then drain and roughly chop. Place in a food processor and blitz until finely chopped, then add the softened butter and blitz again until totally combined. Add the lemon juice and blitz once more. You can keep this in the freezer if you don't use it all here.

Open up the belly of the mackerel and slide a sharp knife in under the rib cage, flicking the bones away from the flesh. Snip the bones at the head end and tail end, then lift out the whole rib cage and any bones. Open the mackerel out slightly, then spoon the dulse butter down the centre, reserving just one large spoonful.

Cut two double-thickness rectangles of foil a little larger than each mackerel and place on a heavy baking tray. Turn up the edges all the way round to make foil trays. Lay the mackerel on the foil and place under the grill to cook while you cook the vegetables – the turned-up edge stops any of the butter running away.

Pour 100ml of water into a sauté pan and bring to the boil. Add the shallot and broad beans, and simmer for 2 minutes. Add the peas and podded peas, and simmer for 1 minute, then add the asparagus and tarragon, and return to a simmer.

Add the last spoonful of dulse butter and cook for 2 minutes, until all the vegetables are tender and the butter is emulsified. Season with a little pepper.

Lift the mackerel out of the trays onto serving plates, pouring any excess butter over the top, and spoon the vegetable stew alongside.

Salt baked sea bass with warm artichoke and bacon salad

Salt baking produces a wonderful taste and keeps the flesh of the fish nice and moist. You do need good sea salt for the job, though – mixed with the egg whites it creates a cocoon around the fish so that it steams inside.

Serves 4–6

4 egg whites

3 lemons

2 bunches of fresh basil, leaves torn

1.25kg sea salt

1 x 2kg whole sea bass, scaled, gutted and cleaned

1 tablespoon vegetable oil

200g smoked back bacon, cut into lardons

600g cooked new potatoes

½ red onion, finely sliced

280g jar of roasted artichokes in olive oil

sea salt and freshly ground black pepper

Preheat the oven to 200°C/400°F/gas mark 6 and line a large baking tray (big enough for the fish) with silicone paper.

Whisk the egg whites in a large bowl until foamy, then add the zest of 2 of the lemons. Chop half the basil and add to the mixture, then add the salt and mix really well to combine.

Slice one of the zested lemons and place in the cavity of the fish along with half of the remaining the basil.

Take one-third of the salt mixture and lay it over the centre of the baking tray, then place the fish on top. Cover with the remaining salt mixture to cover the fish totally. Bake for 30 minutes, or until the crust is golden-brown and the fish is cooked. Push the tip of a knife into the centre to see if the fish is cooked – it should be hot through. Remove and leave to rest for 15 minutes while you make the salad.

Heat a frying pan until hot, add the vegetable oil and bacon, and fry for 3–4 minutes until golden brown and just crispy at the edges. Tip into a serving bowl, then add the potatoes to the pan and fry until hot through and browned at the edges. Add to the bowl, then add the red onion, artichokes and all their oil, and the last of the basil. Season well with plenty of pepper and toss together.

Carefully remove the salt crust from the sea bass and brush any excess salt away from the skin, then carefully lift some of the fish onto each serving plate. Serve with lemon wedges and a spoonful of salad.

Classic individual cheese soufflés

There are loads of hints and tips for making the best soufflé and I'm going to give you a few more. Butter the mould well, including all the way up the sides, and make sure the egg whites are fully whipped and folded into the mixture carefully but quickly. Good luck!

Serves 4

25g unsalted butter, plus extra
    for greasing
25g freshly grated Parmesan cheese
25g plain flour
300ml milk
75g mature Cheddar cheese, grated
75g Gruyère cheese, grated
1 teaspoon Dijon mustard
sea salt and freshly ground pepper
4 eggs, separated
dressed green salad, to serve

Preheat the oven to 180°C/350°F/gas mark 4.

Butter four small ramekins, brushing the butter around the base, then up the sides in straight lines – this will help the soufflé rise. Divide the Parmesan between the ramekins and roll around the inside to coat the sides, then tip out any excess and set aside to add to the sauce later.

Heat a frying pan until hot. Add the butter, and when it's melted, add the flour and cook for 3–4 minutes until a light golden-brown colour. Add the milk in a steady stream, stirring all the time until you have a thick, smooth sauce, then continue to cook for 4–5 minutes at a gentle simmer.

Stir in the Cheddar and Gruyère, any excess Parmesan cheese and the mustard, then remove from the heat and season to taste with salt and pepper. Beat the egg yolks into the mixture and set aside.

Make sure your bowl and whisk are very clean, free of grease and completely dry, as any water or grease will affect the meringue. Place the egg whites in the bowl and whisk to soft peaks with a food mixer or an electric whisk on high speed.

Add half the egg whites to the cheese mixture and whisk firmly to combine, then gently fold in the remaining egg whites, keeping as much air in the mixture as possible.

Spoon into the prepared ramekins, then smooth the top of the mixture with a palette knife, flattening it all the way across. Using the edge of your thumbnail, run your thumb around the edge of the soufflé to move it away from the rim of the ramekin slightly – this will help it rise.

Put the ramekins into a deep-sided roasting tray, then half-fill the tray with hot water and place in the oven for 8–10 minutes until risen and wobbly.

Serve immediately with a little dressed green salad.

Lavender leg of lamb in hay

Unusual I know, but pet shop hay is best for this, as what it produces is an earthy flavour. It's great with lamb and chicken. If you like, you can use a shoulder of lamb rather than a leg, but it will need longer, slower cooking at a lower temperature.

Serves 6–8

1 x 2.7kg whole long leg of lamb
a small handful of fresh picked lavender
½ bag of eating hay (from a pet shop)
50g softened unsalted butter
sea salt and freshly ground black pepper
10 King Edward potatoes, peeled and cut into 2 or 3 pieces
75g beef dripping or vegetable oil
75ml malt vinegar
25g caster sugar
1 large bunch of mint, leaves picked, finely chopped
400g purple-stemmed broccoli

Preheat the oven to 180°C/350°F/gas mark 4. Pierce the leg of lamb about 10–12 times with the point of a knife, then push pieces of lavender into the holes.

Put the hay into a large deep-sided roasting tray, big enough to take the lamb, and sprinkle the rest of the lavender over the top. Place the lamb on the hay, then smear the softened butter over the top, and season with salt and pepper. Cover with foil and place in the oven for 2–3 hours, until cooked to your liking. Remove and leave to rest for at least 30 minutes.

Meanwhile, put the potatoes into a large saucepan, cover with water, add a pinch of salt and bring to the boil. Reduce the heat and simmer for 2 minutes, then drain in a colander and shake around to fluff up the edges.

When the lamb has about an hour left to cook, put the beef dripping into a large roasting tray and tip the potatoes on top. Sprinkle with salt and place in the oven for 30 minutes, until starting to turn golden-brown and crisp. Turn the potatoes and return them to the oven for a further 20–30 minutes.

Heat the vinegar and sugar in a saucepan until simmering, then remove from the heat and stir in the chopped mint.

When ready to serve, bring a pan of salted water to the boil, add the broccoli and simmer for 2–3 minutes until just tender. Drain, and season with salt and pepper and a knob of butter.

Lift the lamb from the hay, then carve and serve with the roast potatoes, mint sauce and broccoli.

Rump steak with creamy brioche leeks

Rump steak is a chef's favourite, as it's full of flavour. My advice is to buy the best quality you can, as there are cheap rump steaks that even your dog would find hard to chew.

Serves 4

1 medium potato, peeled and cut into 1cm dice

sea salt and freshly ground black pepper

125g unsalted butter

1 shallot, finely diced

2 garlic cloves, finely chopped

500g leeks, washed and sliced

100ml white wine

250ml double cream

3 sprigs of thyme, leaves picked

3 slices of brioche loaf, cut into 1cm cubes

50g Gruyère cheese, finely grated

4 x 250g rump steaks

1 tablespoon rapeseed oil

Preheat the oven to 200°C/400°F/gas mark 6.

Bring a pan of water to the boil. Add the potatoes and a pinch of salt, reduce the heat and simmer for 3–4 minutes, then drain.

Meanwhile, heat a frying pan until just warm. Add 50g of the butter and when it's melted, add the shallot, garlic and leeks and cook for 2–3 minutes, or until softened.

Add the potatoes to the pan and mix to combine, then add the white wine and bring to a simmer. Add the cream and thyme leaves, and simmer for 2–3 minutes. Season to taste with salt and pepper and pour into an ovenproof dish.

Heat a separate frying pan until hot. Add 50g of the butter and the brioche cubes and fry until golden-brown on all sides. Scatter over the top of the leeks, then scatter the cheese over the top to cover.

Bake for 5–10 minutes until golden and bubbling.

Meanwhile, heat a griddle pan until searing hot and rub the steaks with the rapeseed oil. Brush the griddle with a little rapeseed, then add the steaks and cook for 2 minutes without moving them. Turn them 90° and cook for another minute. Season with salt and pepper. Turn the steaks over and cook for 1–2 more minutes, then remove from the pan and place on a plate to rest.

Melt the remaining butter in the brioche pan and brush it over the steaks, spooning any resting liquid back over the meat, then season once more.

Serve the steaks with the leeks alongside and any juices poured over them.

Roast grouse with pear tatin and kale

The king of all game birds, the grouse is available from 12th of August – the glorious 12th, as it's called. The key to cooking all game is not to overcook it and to allow it to rest before serving and carving.

Serves 6

150g caster sugar

1 lemon

3 pears, peeled but left whole

100g unsalted butter

100g ready-made all-butter puff pastry

6 grouse, cleaned

sea salt and freshly ground black pepper

500g celeriac, peeled and cut into small chunks

4 sprigs of thyme, leaves picked

75ml port

200ml reduced chicken stock (start with 400ml and simmer until reduced to 200ml)

300g kale, stalks removed

Preheat the oven to 200°C/400°F/gas mark 6. Butter a six-hole muffin tin or silicone muffin mould.

Half-fill a medium saucepan with water and add 75g of the sugar. Squeeze in the lemon juice, then add the squeezed halves to the pan. Add the pears and bring to a simmer. Poach for 15 minutes until tender, then leave until cool enough to handle.

While the pears cool, make the caramel for the tatin. Put the remaining 75g of caster sugar into a frying pan and heat gently, without stirring, until the sugar turns golden-brown and liquid. Add a knob of butter and swirl around the pan, then remove from the heat and divide between the holes in the muffin tin. Roll the caramel around the bases of the holes and set aside to cool slightly.

Slice two thick discs off of the bottom of each of the pears and set them on top of the caramel. Cut six discs of pastry, each 1cm bigger than the holes of the muffin tin. Prick the pastry with a fork, then place over the pears, tucking the excess pastry in around the edges. Bake for 10–15 minutes until the pastry is golden-brown and cooked through. Remove the tatins from the oven and leave to rest for 1 minute before turning out. Place a large serving plate or baking tray over the top of the muffin tin and turn it over, so that the tarts slip out.

Season the grouse inside and out with salt and pepper. Heat a large frying pan until hot, then add a knob of butter and fry the grouse, breast-side down, until golden-brown on the crown and legs. Set them on their backs in a roasting tray, then scatter the celeriac and thyme around the grouse and roast for 15–20 minutes. The grouse should still be pink.

Place the grouse and celeriac on a plate to rest and put the roasting tray on the heat. Add the port and bring to the boil, then simmer until reduced by half. Add the chicken stock and return to the boil, then cook gently for 10 minutes until reduced just by one-third. Pour through a sieve into a clean pan, whisk in a knob of butter and season to taste.

Heat a frying pan until hot. Add the last of the butter, a splash of water and the kale, and sauté for a couple of minutes until just wilted. Season with salt and pepper.

Spoon the celeriac down the centre of each serving plate and top with the kale. Carve the legs and breasts from the grouse and cut the breasts in half. Place the tatin next to the grouse and drizzle with the port sauce.

Layered sole with langoustines and cauliflower

A bit fancy, but this is a dish to show off with. Amazing langoustines and fresh sole are some of the best foods from around the UK. The strange thing is that we export almost all of them to the French and Spanish!

Serves 4

4 sole, filleted and skinned
275ml double cream
sea salt and freshly ground black pepper
1 cauliflower
1 hard-boiled egg, peeled
1 tablespoon finely chopped chives
1 tablespoon white balsamic vinegar
3 tablespoons extra virgin olive oil
16 cooked langoustines, peeled
fennel fronds, to garnish

Trim the sole fillets so that they are all the same size, then set aside (you will have 16 fillets in all, four per fish). Place four of the fillets and the trimmings into a small food processor with 75ml of the double cream, blitz to a fine paste, then season with salt and pepper, and pulse once more. Place in a piping bag and snip the end off the bag.

Lay four of the trimmed fillets on individual sheets of clingfilm twice their size, season with salt and pepper, then pipe a thin layer of the purée on top of each one. Top each one with another fillet and repeat with another layer of purée, then add a final fillet. You will have three layers of fillet with two layers of purée in between. Wrap the clingfilm around the sole so that you have four clingfilm-wrapped parcels, and place in the fridge until ready to cook.

Cut the cauliflower in half. Set one half aside and chop the other half into small florets. Put half the florets into a saucepan with the remaining 200ml of cream and bring to the boil. Turn the heat down and simmer for 4–5 minutes until soft, then tip straight into a blender and blitz to a fine purée. Season with salt and pepper and set aside.

Bring a pan of salted water to the boil and add the rest of the cauliflower florets. Simmer for 2–3 minutes until just tender, then drain.

Finely grate the other half of the cauliflower into a bowl, then grate the hard-boiled egg in too. Add the chives and mix together.

Whisk the white balsamic vinegar and olive oil together in a separate bowl, then spoon two-thirds of this over the salad and toss to coat. Season with salt and pepper.

Set a steamer on top of a pan of simmering water and add the sole parcels. Cover and steam for 6–8 minutes until just cooked through. Lift out and remove the clingfilm.

Add the cauliflower florets and langoustines to the rest of the dressing and toss gently to coat.

Spoon the cauliflower salad in a line across each plate, then place four langoustines along the top. Spoon the purée to one side and set one of the sole parcels on top of it. Place a few cauliflower florets around the langoustines and finish with a drizzle of dressing and some fennel fronds.

Morel mushrooms en cocotte with duck egg

Wild mushrooms are one of the joys of autumn, and cooked this way their taste stays fresh and clean. I love the simple nature of this dish and it's a perfect home comforts recipe. You can use smoked salmon on the base instead of mushrooms, if you wish.

Serves 4

25g unsalted butter
2 shallots, finely chopped
150g morel, wild or field mushrooms, cleaned and roughly chopped
sea salt and freshly ground black pepper
1 tablespoon finely chopped chives
1 teaspoon truffle oil
200ml double cream
4 duck eggs
crusty bread and a dressed green salad, to serve

Preheat the oven to 180°C/350°F/gas mark 4 and butter four ovenproof ramekins.

Heat a frying pan until hot. Add the butter and when it's foaming, add the shallots, mushrooms and a pinch of salt, and fry for 2–3 minutes until wilted and nearly all the moisture has evaporated. Remove from the heat and stir in the chives and half the truffle oil, then season well with salt and pepper. Set aside while you prepare the cream.

Pour the cream into a jug, add the remaining truffle oil, and season well with salt and pepper.

Place the ramekins in a deep-sided roasting tray and divide the mushrooms equally between them. Crack an egg into each ramekin and pour the cream over the top to

cover. Fill the tray with warm water until it comes halfway up the ramekins, then place in the oven for 15–20 minutes until the eggs are just cooked through.

Remove from the tray and place on serving plates. Serve with crusty bread and a dressed green salad.

Deep-fried aubergine with halibut and miso

The idea for this came from a trip to the Indian Ocean – weird, I guess, considering none of the ingredients comes from there. I've added the fish to make it a main course, but this is also a great vegetarian dish made with just the aubergines as a base. You do need to keep an eye on the sauce as it simmers – because of the sugar it can burn easily.

Serves 4

150ml white miso

150g caster sugar

vegetable oil, for deep-frying

2 aubergines, cut into 1–2cm cubes

2 tablespoons roughly chopped coriander

50g unsalted butter

500g halibut fillets, skinned, pin-boned and cut into 8 chunks

100g edamame beans

1 tablespoon white sesame seeds

1 tablespoon black sesame seeds

2 tablespoons mixed micro cress – red amaranth and bronze fennel fronds

Put the miso and sugar into a saucepan with 50ml of water and bring to the boil. Reduce the heat and simmer gently for 10 minutes until thickened and just darkened in colour. Decant into a squeezy bottle fitted with a small nozzle lid – it can be kept like this in the fridge for one week.

Heat a deep-fat fryer to 180°C/350°F, or heat the oil for deep-frying in a deep heavy-based frying pan until a breadcrumb sizzles and turns brown when dropped into it. (CAUTION: hot oil can be dangerous. Do not leave unattended.)

Deep-fry the diced aubergine for 2–3 minutes, or until golden brown and crisp. Set aside to drain on kitchen paper, then add the chopped coriander and toss together.

Heat a large frying pan until hot. Add the butter and when it's foaming, add the halibut and fry on each side for 2 minutes, until golden-brown and just cooked through. Add the edamame beans and warm through.

Mix the two types of sesame seeds together.

To serve, place the aubergine on the serving plates, scatter with the edamame beans, then sprinkle the sesame seeds on top. Finish with two pieces of fish and a drizzle of the miso sauce. Garnish with the cress.

Spiced duck breast with umeboshi sauce and steamed bok choi

A simple dish, but it's the umeboshi plums that make it – sour to taste, they cut through the fat in the duck. They are available online but can also be bought in some supermarkets.

Serves 4

1 teaspoon curry powder
1 teaspoon ground ginger
1 teaspoon five-spice powder
2 teaspoons sansho pepper
4 x 175g duck breasts
4 tablespoons clear honey
1 bok choi, root removed and leaves separated
3cm piece of ginger, peeled and finely chopped
1 garlic clove, crushed
1 red chilli, finely sliced
½ red onion, finely sliced
200g umeboshi plums, stoned

Preheat the oven to 200°C/400°F/gas mark 6.

Mix the curry powder, ground ginger, five-spice and sansho pepper together in a bowl, then sprinkle half the mixture over the skin and flesh of the duck breasts.

Place the duck skin-side down in a cold non-stick frying pan and set over a high heat for 3–4 minutes until the fat renders out. Turn the duck over, then drizzle 2 tablespoons of the honey over the skin and place in the oven for 8–10 minutes. When the duck is cooked, remove from the pan and leave on a plate for 8–10 minutes while you prepare the rest of the dish.

Lay the bok choi in a steamer set over a pan of simmering water. Add the ginger, garlic, chilli and red onion, then cover and steam for 5–6 minutes.

Put the plums into a small blender with 1 teaspoon of the remaining spice mix and the remaining 2 tablespoons of honey. Blitz to a fine purée, then pour into a pan and warm through, adding the resting juices from the duck – taste to see if more honey is needed.

Lay the steamed veg on a plate, carve the duck into thick slices and lay alongside, and finish with a dollop of the umeboshi sauce.

Artichoke with smoked bacon fat mayonnaise

Sounds weird, but the dressing does work – lots of chefs are doing this sort of thing now, and some are even using the fat to distill and make drinks such as lamb fat vodka. Odd, I know.

Serves 4

4 globe artichokes

2 lemons, cut in half

sea salt and freshly ground black pepper

100g plain flour

8 rashers of streaky smoked bacon, roughly chopped

2 egg yolks

1 teaspoon Dijon mustard

400ml rapeseed oil

Pull off the tough leaves from each artichoke and cut off the stalks and top of the leaves and discard. Rub each artichoke with the cut side of a lemon to stop them discolouring, then put straight into a bowl of water while you repeat with the other artichokes.

Squeeze the juice from the lemons into a large saucepan, add a pinch of salt and the flour, then fill the pan with cold water. Add the artichokes, set on the heat and bring to the boil. Reduce the heat to a simmer and cook for 15 minutes until tender when pierced with a knife. The flour will rise to the top of the pan and create a crust, keeping the artichokes from discolouring.

While the artichokes cook, make the mayonnaise. Heat a frying pan until hot, then add the bacon and cook over a medium heat until the fat is rendered out and the bacon crispy. Tip into a bowl and allow to cool.

Place the egg yolks and mustard in a food processor, and blend until pale and creamy. With the motor running, pour in the oil in a steady stream, until the mayonnaise is thick, then add the fat from the cooked bacon. Add the crispy bacon pieces, then pulse to combine and break down the bacon a little. Season with a tiny amount of salt and plenty of pepper.

Remove the artichokes and drain upside down on kitchen paper. Allow to cool slightly, then serve with the bacon mayonnaise.

Tandoori king prawns with butter sauce

Cooked on the barbecue or under the grill, there can be few dishes better than this for cooking outside at home. So many people are used to burnt sausages and dry Frisbee burgers, but try these and you won't go back.

Serves 4

For the prawns

1 teaspoon garam masala
½ teaspoon ground cinnamon
1 teaspoon chilli powder
1 teaspoon ground cumin
2 garlic cloves, crushed
5cm piece of ginger, peeled and finely grated
200ml natural yoghurt
500g large tiger prawns, peeled but tails left on
2 lemons, cut in half

For the butter sauce

50g unsalted butter
1 red onion, finely chopped
2 garlic cloves, finely chopped
1 teaspoon ground cumin
1 red chilli, finely chopped
3 ripe tomatoes, roughly chopped
200ml double cream
5cm piece of ginger, peeled and roughly chopped
2 tablespoons roughly chopped coriander leaves
sea salt and freshly ground pepper

Place all the ingredients for the prawns, except the prawns and lemon, into a bowl and whisk to combine. Stir the prawns carefully into the mixture, then cover and place in the fridge to marinate for at least 20 minutes, preferably overnight.

Meanwhile, get a barbecue ready so that the coals are glowing, and make the sauce. Heat a sauté pan until hot, add the butter and red onion, cook for a couple of minutes until softened, then add the garlic, cumin and chilli, and cook for another minute.

Add the tomatoes, cream and ginger, and bring to the boil, then reduce the heat to a simmer and cook for 4–5 minutes until the sauce has thickened slightly and the tomatoes have broken down. Stir in the coriander and season to taste with salt and pepper.

Remove the prawns from the fridge and thread onto four metal skewers.

Cook on the barbecue for 2 minutes on each side until cooked through. Alternatively, preheat the grill to high and place the skewers on a baking tray. Cook for 2–3 minutes, then turn over and cook for a further 2 minutes until cooked through.

Serve the prawns on the skewers, with lemon halves and a dollop of sauce.

Apple and sage porchetta with apple sauce

I love searching for porchetta in the markets in Italy, and to be fair you don't have to search too hard, as it's a staple over there. It can be eaten hot, but for me it's best served cold cut into thin slices. It is a big piece of pork, though, so it needs a fair amount of time in the oven.

Serves 8–10

4kg pork loin with belly attached, all bones removed

sea salt and freshly ground black pepper

4 medium onions, 2 finely sliced and 2 cut into quarters

4 Bramley apples, 1 sliced and 3 peeled and roughly chopped

1 large bunch of sage, leaves picked and roughly chopped

2 lemons

150g unsalted butter

3 carrots, cut into large chunks

2 garlic bulbs, cut in half horizontally

1 bottle of white wine

2–4 tablespoons caster sugar

500g tenderstem broccoli, trimmed

Preheat the oven to 220°C/450°F/gas mark 7.

Season the pork flesh and skin with plenty of salt and pepper and rub it into the pork. Place the pork skin-side down and scatter the sliced onions, sliced apple, sage, lemon zest, 50g of the butter, salt and pepper over the top, pressing down gently.

Starting with the shortest side in front of you, roll the pork up into a long sausage as tightly as possible and secure with string at intervals along the length of it. Make a little noose in the end of the string, then loop it around the pork, pull the string through the noose and pull it tight. Continue down the pork, wrapping the string around, then looping it back through the string, keeping it taut all the time. Tie it at the end to secure it.

Place the quartered onions, carrots and garlic bulbs in a large deep-sided oven tray, then place the pork on top and rub in another 50g of the butter. Pour the white wine into the tray. Roast for 30 minutes, then turn the oven down to 150°C/300°F/gas mark 2 and cook for 3 or even 4 hours.

While the pork roasts, make the apple sauce. Place 20–25ml water, the chopped apples, a squeeze of lemon, 25g of the butter and a little of the sugar in a saucepan, then cover, place over the heat and cook for 4–5 minutes until the apple has broken down. Beat with a spoon until nearly smooth, leaving a few chunks, then season to taste with the rest of the sugar and a little salt.

Remove the pork from the oven and lift it out onto a serving plate to rest for at least 30 minutes before removing the string. Place the tray on the hob over a medium heat, stirring all the time to release the juices stuck to the bottom of the tray. Check the seasoning, then strain through a fine sieve to serve alongside the pork, with a dollop of apple sauce.

Bring a pan of salted water to the boil. Add the tenderstem broccoli and simmer for 3–4 minutes until just tender. Drain and toss with the last 25g of the butter.

Oyster and seafood pie with samphire

I don't know that 'posh' is the right word for this really, as although it uses oysters and lobster, you can get hold of both of these easily nowadays. It does use a fair bit of champagne, but you can always use prosecco instead. The grated potatoes make a great topping – just give them a thorough squeeze to remove any excess water.

Serves 4–6

140g unsalted butter

2 heaped tablespoons plain flour

600ml double cream

350ml champagne

sea salt and freshly ground black pepper

500g salmon, boneless and skinless, cut into chunks

400g smoked haddock, boneless and skinless, cut into chunks

1kg cooked lobster, shelled and cut into chunks

8 oysters, shucked

350g raw king prawns, shelled and deveined

100g samphire

1kg white potatoes, peeled and coarsely grated

3 egg yolks

200g frozen peas

Preheat the oven to 220°C/425°F/gas mark 7.

Put 75g of the butter into a saucepan and heat until melted, then add the flour and cook for 2 minutes until thickened and light golden-brown.

Add the cream gradually, whisking all the time, and cook until thickened and smooth. Pour the champagne in a steady stream into the sauce, still whisking all the time, until thick enough to coat the back of a spoon, then season to taste with salt and pepper.

Place the salmon, smoked haddock, lobster, oysters, prawns and samphire in a large ovenproof dish. Pour the sauce over the top to coat everything.

Put the grated potato into a clean tea towel and squeeze all the liquid from it. Place in a bowl. Melt 50g of the remaining butter in a saucepan, then mix with the potato and egg yolks and plenty of salt and black pepper.

Sprinkle over the top of the fish, then place on a baking sheet in the oven and bake for 30 minutes until golden and hot through.

Bring a pan of salted water to the boil, add the peas and cook for 2–3 minutes until tender. Drain and return to the pan, add the remaining butter and season to taste. Serve with the fish pie.

Indulgent Comforts

Fun, but not for the faint-hearted. The ice cream itself is not tricky at all to make. It uses a simple custard mixture with malted extract as its base. You can make this in an ice-cream machine or alternatively you can do it using the fancy machine I used for the show, where you freeze the mixture first and then blend it. Both achieve a similar end product.

Bourbon glazed monster doughnut with malted milk ice cream

Serves 10–14

For the ice cream

200ml double cream
300ml whole milk
4 teaspoons malted milk powder
6 egg yolks
100g caster sugar

For the doughnut

1kg strong plain flour
100g caster sugar
250g unsalted butter, plus extra for greasing
600ml milk
18g fresh yeast
200g demerara sugar
1 tablespoon ground cinnamon
200g icing sugar
2 tablespoon bourbon whisky

First make the ice cream. Heat the cream, milk and malted milk powder in a saucepan until the powder has dissolved and the mixture is just simmering. Meanwhile, place the egg yolks and caster sugar in a bowl and whisk together, then pour the warm mixture onto them, whisking all the time.

Return the mixture to the saucepan and cook, whisking all the time, until it thickens just enough to coat the back of a spoon. If you have one, pour into a Pacojet container (the mixture should just come to the 'fill here' mark; do not overfill) and place in the freezer for at least 4 hours until frozen solid. Alternatively, if you do not have a Pacojet, transfer the mixture to an ice-cream machine and churn until frozen, then put into a covered container and freeze until needed.

To make the doughnut, put the flour and caster sugar into a kitchen mixer or large bowl. Put 100g of the butter and half the milk into a saucepan and heat gently on the hob until the butter is just melting, then whisk in the yeast. Take off the heat and whisk until the yeast has dissolved – it doesn't want to be warmer than hand hot. Add the rest of the milk to the mixture, then pour onto the flour and mix for 5 minutes on a medium speed until a dough is formed – it needs to be quite soft and sticky between your fingers.

If you're kneading the dough by hand, turn it out onto a floured surface and knead gently for about 5 minutes. Place the dough in a large bowl, cover with clingfilm and leave in a warm place to prove for 1 hour until well risen, spongy and nearly doubled in size.

Butter a round 38cm deep-sided non-stick pan and the outside of an empty 12.5cm diameter tin or pot. Melt the remaining 150g of butter and pour into a large high-sided tray, then mix the demerara sugar and cinnamon together, and tip into another high-sided tray.

Take the risen dough and knead it gently for a couple of minutes until smooth and elastic, then form into a big bun. Using a pair of scissors, snip the dough in the centre to create a gap through to the bottom of the dough. Carefully ease the dough out slightly to form a hole in the centre, then dip it first into the melted butter, covering it on all sides, and then into the cinnamon sugar. Place in the buttered pan and place the small inner tin or pot in the centre.

Cover with clingfilm and leave in a warm place for about 45 minutes, or until the dough is well risen.

Preheat the oven to 180°C/350°F/gas mark 4. Bake for 30 minutes until golden-brown, then remove the inner tin and turn the whole doughnut out onto a large serving platter. Mix the icing sugar and bourbon together in a bowl until smooth, then spoon into a small piping bag and drizzle over the top of the doughnut.

Spoon the ice cream into a serving bowl that will fit into the hole in the centre of the doughnut. Serve immediately!

Banana and maple syrup cake

Chefs are always on the look-out for new and different ingredients, and once they've found something new they generally stick with it for a while. Well, that ingredient for me at the moment is maple syrup. I can't get enough of the stuff. I love it. There are many grades, but get the best you can afford, as you really can taste the difference.

Serves 6–8

4 ripe bananas, peeled and roughly chopped

200ml maple syrup

50ml milk (only if needed and if the bananas are firm)

200g softened unsalted butter, plus extra for greasing

150g caster sugar

4 eggs

2 teaspoons baking powder

100g pecan nuts, roughly chopped

400g plain flour

200ml double cream

Preheat the oven to 170°C/325°F/gas mark 3. Butter, line and flour a 23cm springform cake tin.

Place the bananas in a food processor and blitz until chunky, then add 75ml of the maple syrup (and the milk if needed) and blitz until smooth.

In a large bowl, whisk the butter and sugar together until pale and very soft, then add the eggs one at a time, whisking well in between. Add the baking powder, then fold in the banana mixture, three-quarters of the pecans and finally the flour.

Spoon into the cake tin, then carefully drop the tin from a height of about 15cm onto the work surface twice, to settle the mixture.

Sprinkle the remaining chopped pecans over the top of the cake and bake for 45–60 minutes, until golden, risen and firm to the touch.

Cool in the tin for 10 minutes, then turn out and leave to cool on a wire rack.

While the cake cooks, put the cream and remaining maple syrup into a saucepan and bring to the boil. Boil for 3–5 minutes until reduced and thickened, then set aside to cool completely.

When the cake is cold, spoon the maple glaze over the top of the cake, allowing it to drizzle down the sides slightly. Set aside for 10 minutes, then cut into slices and serve.

Clotted cream scones with strawberry jam

The best advice I can give you when making scones is to eat them when they are as fresh as possible. But it's also important to work the dough very lightly – the less time you handle it for, the better your scones will be. That's another reason why you should make scones by hand rather than using a machine.

Serves 4

225g plain flour, plus extra for dusting
2½ teaspoons baking powder
a pinch of salt
40g unsalted butter, plus extra to serving
75g caster sugar, plus extra for dusting
1 egg, plus 1 egg yolk, lightly beaten, for glazing
50ml milk
50g clotted cream, plus extra to serve
250g good-quality strawberry jam

Preheat the oven to 200°C/400°F/gas mark 6.

Sift the flour, baking powder and salt into a bowl, then add the butter and rub into the flour, creating a fine breadcrumb consistency. Add the sugar and mix well.

Mix the whole egg, milk and clotted cream together, then add to the mixture to form a smooth dough.

On a lightly floured work surface, form the dough into a disc 15cm in diameter and about 2cm thick. Transfer to a baking tray, then cut through into eight triangles as if you were dividing up a cake, but don't separate the dough, just leave the triangles slightly stuck together.

Brush the scones with the beaten egg yolk, taking care not to let any run over the edge. Dust with caster sugar, then bake for 15 minutes, until golden-brown.

Allow to cool slightly, then tear apart and serve while still warm, with strawberry jam, butter and more clotted cream.

Churros with peaches and custard

This is a kind of fried dough pastry that is very similar to choux pastry in an eclair (see page 154), but is deep-fried and rolled in sugar. Churros are very popular in France, Spain, Portugal and South America. It's best to use a star-shaped nozzle to give the churros their distinctive shape – and also so that they can hold in more hot chocolate sauce. Make sure to use fresh oil when you fry the churros so you don't taint their flavour.

Serves 4

For the custard

5 egg yolks
100g caster sugar
250ml milk
250ml double cream
1 vanilla pod, split and seeds scraped

For the peaches

4 peaches, stoned and roughly chopped
25g caster sugar
75g unsalted butter
2 large sprigs of basil, leaves picked and roughly torn

For the churros

vegetable oil, for deep-frying
50g caster sugar, plus extra for dusting
75g unsalted butter
200g plain flour
¼ teaspoon baking powder
1 egg

Start by making the custard. Whisk the egg yolks in a bowl with half the sugar. Put the milk, cream and remaining sugar into a saucepan with the vanilla pod, set over a medium heat and bring to the boil.

When the milk is boiling, pour it onto the egg yolks, whisking all the time, then return the whole mixture to the pan and cook over a gentle heat, whisking occasionally until thick enough to coat the back of a wooden spoon. Strain into a bowl and set aside.

Put the peaches, sugar and butter into a sauté pan with 50ml of water and set over a medium heat. Add the basil leaves, cover and cook for 5–10 minutes until tender and softened. Place in a serving dish.

To make the churros, heat a deep-fat fryer to 150°C/300°F, or heat the oil for deep-frying in a deep heavy-based frying pan until a breadcrumb sizzles and turns brown when dropped into it. (CAUTION: hot oil can be dangerous. Do not leave unattended.)

Bring 250ml of water, the sugar and butter to the boil in a saucepan set over a medium heat. When boiling, add the flour and baking powder, and beat to a smooth batter. Remove from the heat and beat in the egg, continuing to beat until the batter is smooth and shiny.

Place a large star nozzle in a piping bag and fill with half the batter, then pipe directly into the fat fryer or frying pan in lines, cutting by dipping a pair of metal scissors into the hot oil, then snipping through the batter. Cook for 5–6 minutes until golden and crispy, then lift out and drain on kitchen paper. Repeat with the remaining batter. Toss the churros with caster sugar to coat.

Spoon the custard and peaches into separate bowls, then pile the churros on one big plate and tuck in!

Chocolate eclairs

The key to making a good chocolate eclair is to fill it properly. Most people cut open the choux pastry to put the filling in, but then when they eat it all the cream squirts out of the side. If you fill it this way, with the holes in the top, when you cover it with the fondant icing the cream won't escape when you start eating it.

Makes 8–12

For the choux pastry

a pinch of salt
1 teaspoon caster sugar
100g cold unsalted butter, diced
150g good-quality strong flour
4 eggs

For the icing

100g dark chocolate, roughly chopped
150g fondant icing sugar
4 tablespoons cocoa powder
1.2 litres double cream

Preheat the oven to 200°C/400°F/gas mark 6. Line a baking sheet with silicone paper.

To make the choux pastry, put 250ml of water into a pan with the salt, sugar and butter, and bring to the boil. Add the flour in one go and cook for a few minutes, beating all the time, until the mixture comes away from the sides of the pan cleanly and is smooth. It will sound like bacon frying in a pan when it's ready!

Tip the mixture out onto a silicone-lined tray and leave to cool in the fridge for 5 minutes. Transfer to a kitchen mixer or large bowl and beat in the eggs, one at a time, then continue to beat until the mixture is rich and smooth.

Spoon the mixture into a piping bag fitted with a large, plain nozzle, then pipe long eclair shapes onto the prepared baking sheet. Smooth out any bumps with the tip of a wet finger, then sprinkle them with a little water.

Bake for 25–30 minutes, until golden-brown and crisp, then remove from the oven and transfer the eclairs from the baking tray to a wire rack to cool.

To make the icing, put the chocolate into a bowl set over a pan of water and simmer until it has melted. Remove from the heat, add the icing sugar and cocoa powder, and beat together. Add 2 tablespoons of hot water from the saucepan and beat until smooth, then add 3–4 tablespoons more water, a little at a time, until you have a smooth, shiny, pourable icing. Put back over the pan of water, off the heat, and keep warm until ready to use.

Whip the double cream until soft peaks form when the whisk is removed, and spoon into a piping bag. Using the end of a clean, ink-free biro, make a hole in the top of the eclair at either end. Carefully insert the nozzle of the piping bag into each of the holes and fill with the cream.

Dip the eclairs into the fondant chocolate to cover the top evenly and leave to set before serving – if you can wait!

Bread pudding

Milk puddings have fallen out of favour in recent years, which is a real shame as, made well, they can be really great. Don't keep this bread pudding in the fridge though, as it won't taste as good.

Serves 6–8

100g unsalted butter, plus extra
   for greasing
500g sultanas
100g whisky
600ml milk
150g soft light brown sugar
1 orange, zested
2 teaspoons mixed spice
2 teaspoons ground ginger
500g wholemeal bread
2 eggs, beaten
50g demerara sugar

Preheat the oven to 180°C/350°F/gas mark 4. Grease and line the base of a 20cm square cake tin.

Put the sultanas and whisky into a bowl, swirl around, then set aside to soak for 30 minutes.

Put the milk into a saucepan along with the soft light brown sugar and butter, and set over a medium heat. Heat until the butter has melted, then remove from the heat, stir in the orange zest and spices, and leave for another 15 minutes for the sultanas to soften.

Blitz the bread in a food processor until it forms breadcrumbs, then add to the liquid and mix well. Add the eggs and whisk to combine. Pour into the prepared tin and press down lightly into the corners, then sprinkle with the demerara sugar. Bake for 1 hour until golden brown and just set.

Remove from the oven and leave to cool on a wire rack, then turn out and cut into squares to serve.

Orange and rapeseed oil cake with cream cheese frosting

Olive oil cake is nothing new to anyone who is familiar with Italian cooking. It keeps the cake lovely and moist. Rapeseed oil is a great alternative, as it has a slightly milder flavour.

Serves 8–10

5 large oranges
100ml rapeseed oil
4 eggs
450g caster sugar
125g self-raising flour
125g ground almonds
2 teaspoons baking powder
150g cream cheese
150g crème fraîche
25g icing sugar
25g walnut halves, crumbled
1 tablespoon basil cress or tiny basil leaves

Preheat the oven to 170°C/325°F/gas mark 3. Lightly butter a 23cm springform cake tin.

Remove the zest from three of the oranges and set aside, then remove the pith and discard. Roughly chop the flesh, then either place in a saucepan with the rapeseed oil and blitz until puréed with a stick blender, or blitz with the oil in a food blender.

Whisk the orange zest, eggs and 250g of the caster sugar in a food mixer or a large bowl with an electric whisk, until the mixture is very light and ribbons form when the whisk is lifted out.

Mix the flour, ground almonds and baking powder together in a separate bowl.

Fold half the puréed orange into the eggs, then add all the flour and the rest of the puréed orange.

Pour into the cake tin and bake for 1 hour until golden-brown and risen. Check the cake is cooked by inserting a clean skewer or knife into the centre – if it comes out clean, the cake is ready; if not, cook for a further 5 minutes and check once more.

While the cake cooks, prepare the topping. Whisk the cream cheese, crème fraîche and icing sugar together in a bowl until smooth and thickened, and chill in the fridge until needed.

Peel the last two oranges using a vegetable peeler, then slice the peel very finely into julienne. Put 150ml of water into a saucepan with 150g of caster sugar and the julienned orange peel. Bring to the boil and simmer for 8–10 minutes. Strain into a sieve set over a bowl and press through lightly to remove the sugar syrup. You can use this for a salad dressing or in another cake.

Place the last 50g of caster sugar on a plate and toss the julienned orange peel into it, moving it around with your hands to make sure all the strands are coated.

Remove the cake from the oven and allow it to cool in the tin before turning it out and cooling completely on a wire rack.

Spread the frosting over the top of the cooled cake and decorate with crumbled walnut pieces, the candied julienne strips and basil cress.

Without the cress the cake will keep in an airtight container in the fridge for up to one week.

Dark and white chocolate cherry brownies

When I was in the States, I learnt many things: never drive the wrong way down a one-way street as the police don't like it very much, and never say 'kind regards', as they don't know what it means. The recipe for these brownies is another example of some of the very useful knowledge I brought back with me.

Makes 12 pieces

350g dark chocolate (55–60% cocoa solids)
250g unsalted butter
3 large eggs
250g dark soft brown sugar
110g plain flour
1 teaspoon baking powder
150g fresh cherries, stoned and halved
150g white chocolate, roughly chopped
1–2 tablespoons cocoa powder, for dusting

Preheat the oven to 170°C/325°F/gas mark 3. Grease and line a 30 x 23cm traybake or roasting tin.

Put the dark chocolate and butter into a saucepan and heat until melted, stirring so that it doesn't get too hot, then remove from the heat and cool.

Crack the eggs into a kitchen mixer or a large bowl, then add the sugar and whisk until thickened and paler in colour. Whisk in the cooled chocolate mixture, then gently fold in the flour, baking powder and half the cherries. Spoon into the prepared tin, and scatter the remaining cherries and the white chocolate over the top.

Bake for 30–35 minutes, or until the surface is set. The brownie will be cooked when a skewer inserted into the middle comes out with just a little mixture sticking to it.

Place on a wire rack to cool completely in the tin before removing, dusting with cocoa powder and cutting into squares.

As a pastry chef I was used to making Victoria sponges on a daily basis – however, it wasn't until I entered a competition run by the WI while filming a series for the BBC about ten years ago that I realised how difficult it really was. It turned out I'd used the wrong jam, it had the wrong texture and the wrong sugar on top, and I'd filled it with cream – all of which got me disqualified. Rather than a rosette for first, second or third, I got a full A4 list of all my mistakes. Having said that, I like cream in it, I like the wrong jam and I like the wrong sugar on top, and so, although you can't call this a classic Victoria sponge, it tastes pretty good.

Victoria sponge with mixed berries

Serves 6–8

350g unsalted butter, plus extra
   for greasing

350g caster sugar

4 large eggs

½ teaspoon vanilla bean paste

200g self-raising flour, plus extra for
   dusting

375g strawberries, hulled and quartered

300g raspberries

300g blackberries

150g redcurrants, picked

500ml double cream, very lightly
   whipped

1–2 teaspoons icing sugar

Preheat the oven to 180°C/350°F/gas mark 4. Butter and flour two 20cm springform sandwich tins.

Mix the butter and 200g of the caster sugar together with an electric whisk until softened and lightened in colour, then add the eggs, one at a time, beating between additions. Add the vanilla bean paste, then fold in the flour and carefully pour the mixture into the prepared tins. Bake for 20–25 minutes until golden and risen. A skewer inserted into the centre of the cake should come out clean; if not, return it to the oven for a further 5 minutes and repeat.

Turn the cake out onto a wire rack lined with a tea towel and set aside to cool.

Meanwhile, place the remaining 150g of caster sugar in a pan with 150ml of water and bring to the boil. Simmer for 5 minutes until the texture is like glucose, then add all but a handful of berries to the syrup. Mix gently and leave to cool.

When the cake and berries are both cold, place one cake on a serving plate and spoon over a little of the compote. Carefully spoon the whipped cream over the top, then spoon a layer of the compote all over the cream. Gently set the second cake on top and dust with the icing sugar. Garnish with the remaining berries and serve any leftover compote alongside.

This is one of the simplest desserts you'll ever make, as most of the ingredients are already done for you. All you need is whipped cream, a few strawberries, a ready-made sponge flan and a little bit of imagination. Make sure you use a sharp-sided mould so you get a neat, clean edge. The only bit of real work is cutting the sponge flan in half. Best of luck.

Strawberry gateau with homemade candyfloss

Serves 8–10

1 large shop-bought flan case

50ml Drambuie

800ml double cream

1 tablespoon vanilla bean paste

75g icing sugar

400g large strawberries, trimmed and
  cut in half lengthways

125g caster sugar

125g small strawberries

50g each of raspberries, blueberries
  and blackberries

3–4 sprigs of mint

Place a 20–25cm stainless steel ring on the flan case and use it to cut through, discarding the outer sponge. Cut the flan in half widthways so you end up with two thin layers. Place the steel ring on a large flat serving plate, then place one of the sponge layers inside and press down lightly. Sprinkle 2 tablespoons of the Drambuie over the sponge and set aside.

Put the double cream into a bowl with the vanilla bean paste, the remaining Drambuie and 60g of the icing sugar, and whip to semi-firm peaks.

Line the ring with the large strawberry halves, cut-side against the ring. Carefully spoon the whipped cream into the centre and spread out gently to fill the whole ring – adding as much cream as necessary to fill to the top of the strawberries. Place the remaining sponge layer on top and press down lightly.

Remove the ring by carefully warming the edges with a hot cloth or blowtorch and lifting it straight off. Dust the top of the sponge with the remaining icing sugar.

Put the caster sugar into a very clean frying pan and place over a medium heat to caramelise. Once it is caramelised, remove from the heat and place the base of the pan in a bowl or pan filled with cold water to stop the caramel overcooking.

While the caramel is cooling, heat a metal skewer over a flame or on a hob until very, very hot (taking care to hold the skewer with a cloth), then score the top of the sponge in lines to create a diamond-style pattern. Decorate the top with the small strawberries and the mixed berries, and garnish with the sprigs of fresh mint.

To finish, dip a small spoon into the caramel and as the caramel falls off the spoon, twist it around a metal rod or handle (I used a knife sharpener but you could use the rounded handle of any kitchen utensil) to create some curls, then balance them on top of the gateau.

Serve cut into wedges, with pouring cream if needed.

Billionaire's shortbread (or peanut butter caramel shortbread)

It was one of my chefs' ideas to call this billionaire's shortbread — because millionaire's shortbread is simply not a good enough name for this one. It certainly packs a high calorific value. It will definitely keep anyone at home happy for a few hours, as they won't be wanting anything else.

Serves 6–8

For the shortbread

250g softened unsalted butter, plus extra for greasing
150g caster sugar
1 medium egg
150g cornflour
300g plain flour

For the topping

300g caster sugar
175ml double cream
275g crunchy peanut butter
400g dark chocolate, roughly chopped

Preheat the oven to 180°C/350°F/gas mark 4. Grease and line the base and sides of a 30 x 23cm traybake tin.

To make the shortbread, mix the butter and sugar together in a bowl with an electric whisk until softened and lightened in colour. Add the egg and whisk together, then fold in the cornflour and plain flour to form a soft dough.

Tip the dough out onto a lightly floured work surface and knead very gently until smooth. Press into the base of the prepared tin, spreading it evenly into the corners. Prick all over with a fork, then place in the fridge to rest for 15 minutes.

Bake for about 25 minutes until just lightly coloured and firm to the touch.

Meanwhile, make the topping. Put the caster sugar into a frying pan and heat gently, without stirring, until the sugar turns golden-brown and liquid. Whisk in the cream and cook until thickened and smooth, then whisk in the peanut butter — you want a thick, light golden-brown mixture. Remove from the heat and leave to cool until the shortbread is out of the oven.

Pour the caramel over the shortbread, spreading it to the edges so there's an even layer, then set aside to cool for at least 1 hour.

Put the chocolate into a bowl set over a pan of simmering water until it has melted. Pour three-quarters of the chocolate over the cooled caramel topping, tipping the tray so that it coats all the caramel. Set aside at room temperature to cool for 30 minutes, then drizzle the remaining chocolate over the top. Set the tray aside until the chocolate has set — at least 1 hour.

Lift the shortbread out of the tin by the edge of the silicone paper, and cut into triangles to serve.

Sweet Comforts

Sticky toffee roulade

This is an even more indulgent version of classic sticky toffee pudding, with a hint of bourbon in the sauce. It has a deep flavour and rich colour – exactly what you want from a sticky toffee pudding.

Serves 6–8

For the sponge

150g dates, roughly chopped
4 eggs, separated
75g soft dark brown sugar
1 teaspoon vanilla extract
½ teaspoon bicarbonate of soda
100g plain flour
1–2 tablespoons caster sugar, for sprinkling

For the sauce

200ml double cream
200g unsalted butter
200g soft dark brown sugar
50ml bourbon

Preheat the oven to 230°C/450°F/gas mark 8. Grease and line a 35 x 25cm Swiss roll tin.

Put the dates and 225ml of water into a saucepan, set over a low heat and bring to the boil.

Meanwhile, whisk the egg yolks and dark brown sugar in a kitchen mixer or a large bowl with an electric whisk, until the sugar has dissolved, then set aside.

Pour the dates and water into a blender and blitz to a fine purée.

Whisk the egg whites in a large bowl with an electric whisk until soft peaks form.

Now you're ready to put it all together you need to work quickly. Add the vanilla extract to the sugar and egg mixture, then add the bicarbonate of soda and puréed dates, and mix together. Fold in the flour and mix to combine, then beat in half the egg whites for 10 seconds. Beat in the remaining egg whites until fully incorporated.

Pour straight into the Swiss roll tin and smooth to the edges, then bake in the oven for 11–12 minutes until risen and golden-brown.

While the cake bakes, make the sauce. Put the cream, butter, brown sugar and bourbon into a saucepan set over a medium heat. Bring to the boil, whisking until smooth, then simmer for a few minutes until thickened.

Set a damp clean tea towel on a work surface and dust with the caster sugar. When the cake comes out of the oven, turn it top-down onto the damp tea towel and peel off the lining paper. Spoon one-third of the sauce over the sponge and gently roll the sponge up from the short side to form a fat roll.

Transfer to a serving platter, then spoon some more of the sauce over the top, and serve with the rest of the sauce alongside in a jug.

Chocolate and cherry jam Swiss roll

Swiss roll is the food of many people's childhood, and this one, made with cherry jam and chocolate, brings back so many memories for me. You need a good recipe to make Swiss roll properly – and a good recipe has a reduced amount of flour, which enables the sponge to be rolled more easily without cracking. You can help it along by using a damp tea towel; the steam that will come off the tea towel will slightly softens the sponge.

Serves 6–8

5 eggs
125g caster sugar, plus extra for dusting
1 vanilla pod, seeds scraped out
75g self-raising flour
20g cocoa powder
200g cherry jam
75g dark chocolate
1 tablespoon kirsch

Preheat the oven to 190°C/375°F/gas mark 5. Line a 25 x 38cm Swiss roll tin with baking parchment.

Place the eggs, sugar and the seeds from the vanilla pod in a bowl and whisk with an electric whisk until very light, fluffy and thickened. Fold the flour and cocoa into the mixture using your hand, carefully lifting and mixing until it is all incorporated.

Pour into the prepared tin and smooth with a spatula until evenly spread out. Bake for 10–12 minutes, or until just firm to the touch.

Place a damp wrung-out clean tea towel that is slightly bigger than the tray on a work surface and dust with caster sugar. Turn the sponge out onto the tea towel, then peel off the parchment on the bottom of the sponge. Starting at the shortest edge nearest you, roll the sponge up in the tea towel, pressing gently as you go, then unroll.

Gently warm the jam in a saucepan until runny, then stir in the kirsch.

Using a potato peeler, shave the chocolate over the sponge to cover it completely, then spread the warm cherry jam over the top, leaving a 2cm border at the furthest short edge.

Take the nearest short edge and, using the tea towel underneath, roll up the sponge quite tightly, making sure the filling stays inside.

Roll the sponge off the tea towel, straight onto a plate, and serve straight away, cut into thick slices.

English apricot and almond bake

When you make the frangipane, make sure to mix the butter and sugar together until they are white, and then fold in the flour by hand to help keep it as light as possible. It's best not to keep the bake in the fridge, as the butter will harden up – if you have to, warm it through in a low oven before serving.

Makes 15 pieces

375g shop-bought sweet pastry
200g unsalted butter, softened
200g caster sugar
3 large eggs
200g plain flour
125g ground almonds
½ teaspoon baking powder
150g apricot jam
8 fresh apricots, stoned and quartered

Preheat the oven to 170°C/325°F/gas mark 3. Grease and line a 30 x 23cm traybake tin.

Roll out the pastry to 5mm thick and about 2cm larger than your tin. Roll it onto the rolling pin, then roll it over the tin. Press gently into the corners, then trim the excess from the edges. Place in the fridge while you make the filling.

Place the butter and sugar in a food mixer or a large bowl, and beat for 5 minutes until light and fluffy, then beat in the eggs one at a time. Remove from the mixer and fold in the flour, ground almonds and baking powder.

Cover the pastry with the apricot jam, then spoon over the filling and smooth out to the edges. Lay the apricot halves gently on top, in rows, and bake for 35–40 minutes until golden-brown and risen. A skewer inserted into the centre of the cake should come out clean; if it doesn't, return it to the oven for a further 5 minutes and repeat.

Leave the cake to cool in the tin, then cut into rectangles to serve.

Chocolate and salted caramel banoffee cheesecake

One of the best cheesecakes I've ever tasted was in New York, at Eileen's Special Cheesecake bakery. All she sells is cheesecakes, in all manner of sizes and flavours. The bakery where she makes them is at one end, the shop is at the other end, and the queue outside is immense.

Serves 2

100g full-fat cream cheese
100ml crème fraîche
125ml double cream
1 vanilla pod, split and seeds scraped
50g dulce de leche
½ teaspoon sea salt
40g caster sugar
25g unsalted butter
2 bananas, peeled
2 chocolate digestive biscuits
25g dark chocolate

Put the cream cheese, crème fraîche, 75ml of the double cream and the vanilla seeds into a bowl and whisk until well combined.

Put the dulce de leche and salt into a bowl, and whisk together, then lightly fold into the cream mixture until just marbled through. Set aside.

Heat the sugar in a frying pan until golden and liquid, then add the bananas and coat in the caramel. Whisk in the butter and the rest of the cream and coat once more.

Crumble each biscuit onto a serving plate, place the caramel-coated bananas on top, drizzle the sauce around, and finish with a quenelle of dulce de leche cream. Finally, grate the chocolate over the top.

Elderflower jelly with peaches and strawberry with quick strawberry ice cream

Jelly and ice cream make such a perfect combination. Even this grown-up version made with elderflower cordial reminds me of when I was young, when my mother would serve me jelly and ice cream when I was poorly. It's easier to get the right amount of gelatine if you use the leaf form, as the powdered type sometimes doesn't dissolve properly and you can end up with too much – resulting in a jelly that has set too firm.

Serves 4

For the jelly

450ml sparkling elderflower pressé
50g caster sugar
5 sheets of leaf gelatine, soaked in
  cold water
1 peach, stoned and finely diced
50g small strawberries, quartered
a small handful of Greek basil

For the ice cream

500g strawberries, hulled
½ vanilla pod, seeds scraped
300ml thick double cream

To make the jelly, heat 100ml of the sparking elderflower pressé and the caster sugar in a saucepan until hot, then add the soaked gelatine and stir gently until it has dissolved. Add the rest of the elderflower pressé and stir to combine.

Pour the jelly into a soup plate or lipped plate and place in the fridge for 30 minutes to set.

To make the ice cream, place the strawberries in a sealable food bag and freeze for at least 4 hours, but preferably overnight. When they're frozen and you're ready to serve the jelly, tip the strawberries into a food processor with the vanilla seeds and half the cream, and blitz until they start to break down. Continue blitzing for 3–4 minutes until it becomes smoother, then add the remaining cream and blitz until it forms a smooth frozen cream.

With the jelly still in the plate, lay a line of chopped peaches down one side of the jelly, then top them with the strawberries and Greek basil. Place spoonfuls of the ice cream in a line alongside and serve immediately, with the remainder of the ice cream in a separate bowl.

Raspberry rabbit blancmange

In this recipe I've added both raspberries and blended raspberries to a traditional sweet blancmange. A bit of fun, the rabbit moulds are something my grandma used to use when she made blancmange, although she used a packet mix. It makes a great, different dessert for a dinner party – and I think that's what doing dinner parties is all about: serving the unexpected.

Serves 4

750g raspberries
100g icing sugar
5 sheets of leaf gelatine
1 heaped tablespoon cornflour
250ml full-fat milk
1 teaspoon vanilla extract
250ml double cream
2–3 sprigs of lemon verbena, leaves picked

Place 600g of the raspberries and all but 2 tablespoons of the icing sugar in a blender and blitz to a purée, then pass through a fine sieve into a bowl, discarding the seeds.

Soak the gelatine in a bowl of cold water for a few minutes until softened.

Mix the cornflour and the remaining 2 tablespoons of icing sugar with 75ml of the milk to form a smooth paste, then stir in the remaining milk and the vanilla extract. Pour into a saucepan and heat until just simmering and thickened slightly, then add the soaked squeezed gelatine and heat until dissolved, stirring constantly.

Remove from the heat, whisk in the double cream, then add 150ml of the raspberry purée and whisk to combine. Pour into the rabbit moulds (1 large and 1 small, or whatever you have to hand), then transfer to the fridge and leave to set for 4 hours.

Thirty minutes before serving, remove the moulds from the fridge and leave at room temperature before turning out. Dip into a bowl of hot water very quickly to loosen, then invert onto a serving plate. Blowtorch the rabbit blancmanges very lightly, until just shiny, and serve with the remaining raspberry purée, the rest of the raspberries and the lemon verbena leaves.

Apple milk pancakes with roasted apples, pears and walnuts, and a vanilla syrup

Pancakes should always be in any book of home comfort recipes. They are so simple to make and they also freeze really well – these ones included. Once you've made them, layer them between sheets of greaseproof paper and pop them into the freezer. To use them, allow them to defrost and then reheat.

Serves 4

For the pancakes

100g plain flour

40g caster sugar

1 teaspoon baking powder

3 eggs

100ml almond milk

2 tablespoons vegetable oil

For the apples and pears

2 apples, cut into chunks

2 pears, cut into chunks

4 tablespoons honey

75g walnuts

For the vanilla syrup

1 teaspoon vanilla bean paste

100g caster sugar

100ml almond milk

To make the pancakes, place the flour, sugar and baking powder in a bowl and whisk until combined. Make a hollow in the centre, then crack in the eggs and pour in the almond milk. Whisk gently from the centre outwards until all the flour is taken in and you have a smooth batter.

Heat a frying pan until hot, then add the vegetable oil and a large spoonful of batter. Fry over a medium heat until golden-brown and little bubbles have appeared over the surface, then flip and cook for a further minute until cooked through. Set aside and repeat with the remaining batter.

Heat a frying pan until hot and add the apples and pears. Fry for 2–3 minutes, then add the honey and 4 tablespoons of water and bring to the boil. Toss the apples and pears to coat, then add the walnuts.

For the vanilla syrup, put the vanilla bean paste, sugar and almond milk into a saucepan, and bring to the boil, then reduce the heat slightly and simmer until thickened.

Divide the pancakes between the plates, then surround with the apple mixture and drizzle with the syrup

Individual hot chocolate and hazelnut mousse cake with pouring cream

This simple little dish contains no flour at all, so it's the perfect dessert if you are gluten-intolerant or need it to be gluten-free. Make sure to serve it at room temperature or while it is still warm, as it will go very hard in the fridge because of its lack of flour.

Serves 6

60g chopped toasted hazelnuts
200g dark chocolate
100g unsalted butter
4 eggs, separated
50g caster sugar
250ml pouring cream, to serve

Preheat the oven to 180°C/350°F/gas mark 4. Line the bases of a six-hole large muffin tin with discs of silicone paper.

Blitz the toasted hazelnuts to a powder in a food processor or blender and set aside.

Put the dark chocolate and butter in a bowl set over a saucepan of simmering water and heat until melted, stirring so that it doesn't get too hot, then remove from the heat and cool slightly.

Put the egg yolks into a bowl with half the sugar and set over the pan of simmering water. Whisk until thickened and pale in colour, then set aside.

Make sure your bowl and whisk are very clean, free of grease and completely dry, as any water or grease will affect the meringue. Place the egg whites in the bowl and whisk with a food mixer or an electric whisk on high speed, to soft peaks. Add the remaining caster sugar, whisking until the mixture is smooth and glossy. You should hear the machine dropping down a gear as it gets to the correct consistency.

Pour the melted chocolate mixture onto the egg yolks and mix to combine, then fold in the ground hazelnuts and half the whisked egg whites. Whisk well to combine, then carefully fold in the rest of the egg whites and divide equally between the muffin tins.

Bake for 8–10 minutes, or until the surface is set – there should still be a wobble. Remove and cool slightly before turning out.

Serve with pouring cream.

Lemon posset with figs, strawberries and Gran's shortbreads

Traditionally, a posset was a hot drink made from curdled milk with wine or ale added to it, and sometimes spiced with nutmeg and cloves. It was often used as a cold or flu remedy. Nowadays, it's more similar to a syllabub. It's amazing how only a few simple ingredients can produce a dessert as intense as this – sharp to the taste and so easy to make.

Serves 4–6

For the posset

600ml double cream
150g caster sugar
2 large lemons, zested and juiced
8 strawberries
2 figs, cut into wedges
a handful of tiny mint sprigs, to garnish

For the shortbread

175g plain flour
90g icing sugar
60g ground almonds
25g cornflour
250g unsalted butter, cut into cubes
200g strawberry jam

First make the posset. Bring the cream and sugar to the boil in a saucepan, then remove from the heat and whisk in the lemon zest and juice. Whisk well, then pour into serving bowls and place in the fridge to set for 1 hour.

Preheat the oven to 180°C/350°F/gas mark 4.

To make the shortbread, mix the plain flour, icing sugar, ground almonds and cornflour together in a bowl. Rub the butter into the flour until it forms a breadcrumb-like texture, then pull together very lightly to form a soft dough.

Divide the dough into small balls and press into a 24-hole silicone bun tin or fairy cake tin. Bake for 10–12 minutes until they are a light golden colour. If you have dough left over, make a second batch. The shortbread mix makes more than you need for this recipe, but keeps well in an airtight tin.

While the shortbreads are baking, put the jam into a saucepan with 50ml of water and bring to the boil. Simmer for a few minutes until it has a thick syrup texture.

Remove the shortbreads from the oven and carefully make a small dent in the centre of each one with your finger, to create a hollow to put the strawberry jam. Spoon the warm jam into the dent and set aside to cool on a wire rack, still in the tin.

Take the posset out of the fridge and decorate with the strawberries, figs and mint sprigs. Serve with the shortbread.

I was first introduced to making meringue roulade by the great Mary Berry, and ever since then I've always made this dessert at home. The cooking times and temperatures are really vital, so that the meringue stays nice and soft and pliable in the centre. If it's too hot, it cracks; if it's too cold, it firms up and you won't be able to roll it.

Lemon and plum meringue roulade

Serves 8–10

5 egg whites

400g caster sugar

2 sprigs of lemon verbena, leaves picked, plus extra to garnish

8 plums, quartered and stoned

400ml double cream

225g good-quality lemon curd

Preheat the oven to 180°C/350°F/gas mark 4. Grease a 35 x 25cm Swiss roll tin and line with silicone paper.

Make sure your bowl and whisk are very clean, free of grease and completely dry, as any water or grease will affect the meringue. Place the egg whites in the bowl and whisk with a food mixer or an electric whisk on high speed, to soft peaks. Add 275g of the caster sugar, whisking until the mixture is smooth and glossy. You should hear the machine dropping down a gear as it gets to the correct consistency.

Spoon the meringue into the prepared tin and spread evenly to the edges using a palette knife, then scatter the lemon verbena over the top. Bake for 8 minutes until golden-brown, then lower the oven temperature to 170°C/325°F/gas mark 3 and bake for a further 10 minutes until crisp.

Remove from the oven and turn out of the tin onto a clean tea towel. Remove the paper from the base of the meringue and allow to cool.

Put the plums into a saucepan with 100g of the sugar and 100ml of water. Bring to the boil, then cook for 10 minutes until the plums are softened.

Whisk the double cream in a large bowl until very soft peaks form, then whisk in the last 25g of the sugar and the lemon curd, and mix gently until it just holds a peak.

Spread the lemon cream over the cooled meringue all the way to the edges, leaving a 1cm gap along one long edge, then spoon three-quarters of the cooked plums over the top. Starting at the long end with the border, roll up the meringue using the tea towel to help you. Roll it carefully off the tea towel onto a serving platter, and decorate with any remaining plums and lemon verbena.

St Emilion is a famous wine region of Bordeaux, and I was fortunate enough to visit it a lot as a young nipper. Not to taste the wine, but because my family used to work over there. In the main square of St Emilion was a macaron shop, and I'd often pop in on the way home. The macarons were cooked and served on cardboard and you'd end up pulling them off with your teeth. Crunchy on the outside and soft in the middle, good macarons are a real joy.

St Emilion macarons

Serves 2, plus extra macarons

For the macarons

100g icing sugar
100g ground almonds
100g caster sugar
50ml water
2 egg whites

For the chocolate mousse

150g good-quality plain chocolate, broken into pieces
40g unsalted butter, melted
4 eggs, separated
50g caster sugar
150ml good-quality red wine, ideally St Emilion or Merlot

Preheat the oven to 130°C/260°F/gas mark ¾ and line two baking sheets with silicone paper. Make 24 circles, 4.5cm in diameter – this is your template for piping. Flip the paper over so the pencil line is on the underside but the outline can still be seen.

Place the icing sugar and ground almonds in a food processor and blitz to a fine powder, scraping down the sides halfway through, then set aside.

Put the caster sugar and 50ml of water into a saucepan and bring to the boil. Continue to boil until the mixture reaches 110°C/230°F, or soft boil, on a thermometer.

Make sure the bowl and whisk you are using for the next step are very clean, free of grease and dry, as any water or grease will affect the meringue. Place the egg whites in the bowl and whisk with a food mixer or an electric whisk on high speed until soft peaks form. Add the sugar syrup, whisking until the mixture is smooth and glossy and has cooled slightly, at least 2 minutes.

Transfer half the meringue to a clean bowl, then sieve in the ground almond mixture and whisk together to form a thick paste. Fold in the remaining meringue – you will end up with a smooth, pipeable mixture. Transfer it to a piping bag fitted with a 7mm plain nozzle, and secure the silicone paper to the baking sheets with a dab of the mixture.

Pipe the mixture onto the template so that it just fills each circle – hold the bag upright and press down lightly to fill the circle

before lifting off quickly. Use a wet finger to lightly press the peak down on the macaron, then set aside for at least 30 minutes until the mixture has spread slightly.

Bake for 25 minutes until crusted and risen. Remove from the oven and leave to cool on the baking sheets.

To make the mousse, melt the chocolate and butter together in a bowl set over a pan of simmering water.

Whisk the egg yolks and sugar together in a bowl set over a second pan of simmering water until light and thick. Remove both pans from the heat, but leave the bowls set over the pans of water to keep warm.

Make sure the bowl and whisk you are using for the next step are very clean, free of grease and dry, as any water or grease will affect the meringue. Place the egg whites in the bowl and whisk with a food mixer or an electric whisk on high speed until soft peaks form.

Fill the bottom of two large wine glasses with a few macarons, then divide the red wine between the glasses.

Whisk the warm chocolate mixture into the eggs and sugar, then lift the bowl off of the saucepan and fold in the egg whites, a spoonful at a time, until totally incorporated.

Pour the mousse over the wine-covered macarons, and top each with one more macaron. Put into the fridge to set for a couple of hours before serving.

Queen of puddings

This is a traditional British dessert that you don't often see nowadays, which is sad, as it's very, very simple to make. It has a basic custard mixture as its base, which is spread with jam, topped with meringue, then baked.

Serves 4–6

unsalted butter, for greasing
225ml milk
225ml double cream
1 tablespoon vanilla bean paste
5 eggs, separated
300g caster sugar
150g fresh breadcrumbs
2 lemons, zest only
250g plum jam

Preheat the oven to 150°C/300°F/gas mark 2. Butter a medium-sized ovenproof dish and place it in a large roasting tin.

Heat the milk, cream and vanilla bean paste in a saucepan until just simmering. Meanwhile, put the egg yolks and 100g of the sugar into a large bowl and whisk until light and fluffy. Slowly pour the hot milk and cream onto the eggs, whisking all the time, then fold in the breadcrumbs and lemon zest.

Pour the mixture into the buttered dish, then pour enough hot water into the roasting tin to come halfway up the dish. Place the roasting tin in the centre of the oven and bake for 10–15 minutes until the custard is still slightly wobbly in the centre. Remove and allow to cool slightly, then turn the oven up to 190°C/375°F/gas mark 5.

Make sure the bowl and whisk you are using for the next step are very clean, free of grease and dry, as any water or grease will affect the meringue. Place the egg whites in the bowl and whisk with a food mixer or an electric whisk on high speed until soft peaks form. Add all but one spoonful of the remaining sugar and whisk until shiny and smooth.

Warm the jam in a saucepan until just melted, then spoon over the top of the custard. Spoon the meringue over the jam, sprinkle with the remaining sugar and bake for 8–10 minutes, until the top is crisp and lightly browned. Serve immediately.

Blueberry cobbler with custard

This is an American version of our simple crumble, the difference being that the topping is more like a scone. But as it cooks, the scones separate out to reveal an almost crumble-like topping underneath.

Serves 6

For the filling

500g blueberries
30g vanilla sugar
1 tablespoon plain flour
1 lemon, zested and juiced

For the topping

200g plain flour, plus extra for dusting
1 tablespoon baking powder
50g caster sugar
50g unsalted butter, softened
1 large egg
200ml natural yoghurt
1 tablespoon granulated sugar

For the custard

250ml whole milk
250ml double cream
1 vanilla pod, split, seeds scraped out
100g caster sugar
6 egg yolks

Preheat the oven to 180°C/350°F/gas mark 4. Butter a 15cm x 25cm ovenproof baking dish.

For the filling, tip the blueberries into the baking dish. Add the vanilla sugar, flour, lemon zest and juice, and toss to combine, then set aside.

To make the topping, mix the plain flour, baking powder and sugar together in a bowl, then rub in the butter until it forms a breadcrumb-like texture. Mix the egg and yoghurt together, and stir into mixture until you have a soft, sticky dough.

Tip the dough out onto a lightly floured work surface and knead gently until smooth. Push out into a rough rectangle about 4cm thick, then fold each side into the centre and fold in half, as if shutting a book. Cut the dough into 10 even-sized pieces and place on top of the blueberries – you don't want to handle it too much.

Scatter the granulated sugar over the top and bake for 35–40 minutes until golden and bubbling around the edges.

Meanwhile, make the custard. Put the milk and cream into a shallow saucepan with the vanilla pod, set over a medium heat and bring to the boil. Whisk the sugar and egg yolks in a bowl. When the milk is boiling, pour it onto the eggs, whisking all the time, then return the whole mixture to the pan and cook over a gentle heat, whisking occasionally, until thick enough to coat the back of a wooden spoon.

Strain into a clean pan and warm through when the cobbler is ready.

Fruit meringue gateau

This is a very simple dish. The key is to keep it in the fridge for 3–4 hours before serving. The fruit, cream and meringue start to stick together and the meringue softens up – in a similar way to an Eton mess.

Serves 6–8

6 egg whites
400g caster sugar
1 litre double cream
1 tablespoon vanilla bean paste
500g strawberries, hulled and cut in half
4 plums, halved, stoned and finely sliced
5 figs, cut into small wedges
2 tablespoons toasted flaked almonds

Preheat the oven to 110°C/225°F/gas mark ½. Draw four 20cm circles, using a cake tin as a template, on four sheets of silicone paper. Turn the sheets of paper over, so that the pencil line is on the underside but can still be seen through the paper, and place on four flat baking sheets (or two large, if your oven is big enough.)

Make sure your bowl and whisk are very clean, free of grease and completely dry, as any water or grease will affect the meringue. Place the egg whites in the bowl and whisk with a food mixer or an electric whisk on high speed, to soft peaks. Add 300g of the sugar, continuing to whisk until the mixture is smooth and glossy. You should hear the machine dropping down a gear as it gets to the correct consistency.

Spoon into a piping bag fitted with a 1cm plain nozzle and pipe a little meringue onto the back of each sheet of silicone paper to secure the paper to the tray. Pipe a disc of meringue onto each template, starting in the centre and working out. Flatten the top of the meringue using a wet palette knife to give a smooth top. Place in the oven for 2 hours. Remove from the oven and cool fully before using.

Place the cream and vanilla bean paste in a bowl and whisk with a food mixer, or an electric whisk on high speed, to soft peaks.

Place one disc of meringue on a cake stand or a large serving plate and spread with one-third of the cream, then scatter one quarter of the sliced fruit over the top. Cover with another disc of meringue, then repeat with a layer of cream, more fruit, another meringue disc, then the last of the cream and half the remaining fruit. Finish with the last meringue disc and decorate with the last of the fruit.

Heat the last 100g of caster sugar in a pan until golden-brown and liquid all the way through. Add the flaked almonds and stir to combine, then drizzle over the top of the gateau.

Chill for 3–4 hours before serving.

Index

I would like to thank so many people at this point. First, the guys at my house for putting up with all the mess and putting it back to normal again once the film crew had gone. Thanks to all my friends who took part in the show to make it what it is, and to the food producers for all their work for the show and the book. Thanks to all the TV team, especially Nicola, Sophia and Alex. To Limelight Management, and Fiona, for filling my diary for more than 20 years. To Chris, Janet and David for all their work on and off screen to make the food what it is behind the lens. To Beata, for washing more pots and dishes than a 300-room hotel: you're a star. To all the guys at Quadrille for their amazing work in making and designing another brilliant book. Peter Cassidy, you are the main man behind the lens and your work says it all – mega thanks. Finally to Lou, Fudge and Ralph for keeping me sane and telling me to have a break when I really did need it, and for trying the food for me.